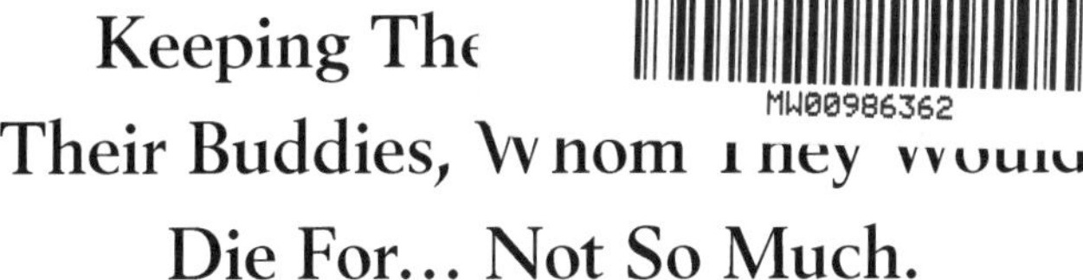

Keeping The Their Buddies, Whom They Would Die For… Not So Much.

Navy SEALs have only two things to watch out for: the bad guys…and their fellow SEALs. Amid the unthinkable pressures these brave men face on their freedom-protecting missions are periods of training and downtime—which leaves all-too-many opportunities for them to figure out practical jokes on their friends and payback on pretty much anyone who has the bad judgment to cross them.

Navy SEALs and Their Unabashed Humor lays bare the mischief real SEALs have gotten into. Thanks to these stories we know:

- To be wary of Aussie commandoes and their cloudy ice cubes
- Why Navy SEALs might go bald
- If you're a SEAL, you're not even safe on the crapper
- Not to trust your SEAL buddies to plan your bachelor party
- It's not smart to play jokes on SEAL wives

Author Billy Allmon, a combat veteran of three wars, has to rank right up there among the best of practical jokers. And he has the stories—and the scars—to prove it.

ABOUT THE AUTHOR

William (Billy) Allmon is a combat veteran of three wars, serving as a Navy SEAL from 1969-1993. He has participated in and led covert operations and classified missions worldwide. His résumé reads like a list of James Bond adventures, and includes boots-on-the-ground activities in many countries, from El Salvador to Desert Storm, where he served as an intelligence officer.

In addition to his battlefield and special operations experience, Billy is recognized as a counter-terrorist and security expert and, at the Maritime University in Long Island, New York, he taught anti-piracy procedures, how to survive as a hostage, and techniques for dealing with stowaways. He has instructed U.S. Navy SEALs in combat tactics, weapons of mass destruction, close-quarters battle, field tracking, scout sniper, unarmed combat, and clandestine communications systems and procedures, among other useful skills. He is regularly contacted by government agencies for his technical expertise in order to better train military technicians and Special Operations Groups prior to their deployments.

Billy retired as a Chief Petty Officer and lives quietly in the desert—where he is almost certainly dreaming up new and more "hilarious" practical jokes to play on his SEAL brothers… or others.

NAVY SEALs AND THEIR UNABASHED HUMOR

NAVY SEALs AND THEIR UNABASHED HUMOR

Unfiltered, Uncensored and Unhinged!

BILLY ALLMON

Beverly Hills, CA

Pippin Publishing
269 S.Beverly Dr
Beverly Hills, California 90212
www.pippinpublishingbooks.com

Printed in the United States of America

Publisher's Cataloguing-in-Publication Data

Allmon, Billy.

Navy SEALs and their unabashed humor / Billy Allmon. -- Beverly Hills, CA : Pippin Publishing, [2015]

pages : illustrations ; cm.

ISBN: 978-0-9787389-0-7
Summary: What's more dangerous than the enemy? To a Navy SEAL, the answer is ... his buddies, when they play practical jokes. SEAL Billy Allmon is a veteran of three wars. But more than that, he is the veteran of countless practical jokes, most of which were perpetrated on the very brothers whose lives he had saved, or they his.--Publisher.

1. United States. Navy. SEALs--Humor. 2. United States. Navy. SEALs --Biography. 3. Allmon, Billy--Anecdotes. 4. American wit and humor. 5. Humor. 6. Anecdotes.

VG87 .A45 2015 2015953477
359.9/840973--dc23 1511

Cover Design: Lewis Agrell
Interior Design: Ghislain Viau

To my wife and good friend, Alice: Thank you for standing by me for better and for worse. We both know that with all of my deployments, I gave you more worse than better.

To my sons: I am so proud of the men that you have become. Never forget, no matter where you go in life or what you do, it is your wife and children who need you the most, and when you are ill or down, it is they who will be by your side.

To all the Frogmen and SEALs out there, I thank you. Without your unique sense of humor, this book would not have been possible. And let me also say to everyone who is or has served in the military, thank you all for your unwavering dedication and service to our country.

CONTENTS

PREFACE

There have been many books written about the U.S. Navy SEALs. However, in this book I want to concentrate on the humorous side of the Navy SEALs. I feel that there are enough books and movies out there about the blood, guts, and gore of combat. Besides, just about every Navy SEAL (and non-SEALs) would much rather laugh than read about, or hear about, catastrophically harmful events.

Anyone who has been in combat, has been a police officer, first responder, firefighter, worked in the ER of a hospital, a burn center, or a cancer ward—those are the kinds of people I feel would much rather laugh than to sit down and read a book about all the stories of pain, fear, and death.

So, what is it about "dark" humor that is funny? Some may feel that the practical jokes within this book are childish, not funny, or even uncalled for, given the situation and the profession that the stories encompass—scenarios in which all Navy SEALs must work. To those people, I say: You are truly blessed for living such a comfortable life. You have been sheltered from all the ugliness that surrounds you.

I would also presume to say that your career is *not* in the field of saving or protecting people's lives within the United States, or in any other country overseas. Consequently, you may lack the exposure to life's ugliness, which would provide you with a keen insight into the kind of understanding that is sometimes needed for gallows humor.

The humor within these pages depicts the raw truth of what it takes to continue on mentally, in a career filled with suffering, death, and fear in order to keep one's sanity intact. Consider yourself to be made aware that the humor contained within these pages is *not* politically correct. It is gross, off-color, sick, or any other word that the faint of heart use because they cannot stomach such humor. So, proceed at your own risk, as you will be demented by SEAL humor.

After my first book, *When the Bullet Hits Your Funny Bone: The Essence of a U.S. Navy SEAL*, I received a few reviews from people who clearly disliked those who served in the military. It made me wonder why they would even bother to purchase a book that was about people who served in the military in the first place.

Although everyone is entitled to their own opinion, I found it amusing that in their reviews, they stated I had lied about the "activities," and the stories, because they could not possibly be true (as if these readers were there), and as if "their review" was the only one that was going to truly matter!

Here is a thought for people who write negative reviews: A few bad reviews are like restaurant reviews; when it comes to certain people, no matter what you serve them, and no matter the quality of the food, atmosphere, or location, it won't matter. Why? Because no matter what it is they are given, they have already made up their minds that they aren't going to like it.

Cheers, and I hope you have the guts to enjoy some SEAL humor!

Billy Allmon
SMC
USN SEAL ret.
Class 58

Chapter 1

TEN-MILE RUN? BRING BUS FARE!

Running was never my forte. I mean, sure, it is necessary, and it is a part of staying in shape while you're in the SEAL teams, but the idea of running in battle, for the most part, is a foolish one. Why? Well, for one, if you have not engaged the enemy, running narrows your field of view. There are other reasons, but I am not here to help the bad guys by giving them tactical information. As a chief in a SEAL platoon, I would tell my guys, "When you engage a superior force without any support fire, you have two choices: You can run until you get tired and then turn around and fight, or you can turn around and fight."

In a Navy SEAL's life, one or two hours of each and every workday are spent working out. Back in the states, and depending on what SEAL team you are assigned to, your

Monday through Friday is comprised of different workout routines. For example:

Monday: Two hours of physical training (PT) exercises

Tuesday: Obstacle course followed by a two-mile run

Wednesday: One-mile ocean swim

Thursday: Three-mile run

Friday: Lumpkin Park to the Blue Inlet run, which is only about ten miles, but because of the heat and humidity, it feels like fifty

I was new to the East Coast at the time, having come from SEAL Team One on the West Coast. East Coast SEALs would call us Hollywood Frogmen or West Coast Pukes, a term of endearment for all West Coast SEALs. One day I asked about the Lumpkin Park run… and I was given this explanation:

"Once you get dropped off at the Lumpkin Park starting point, there is a small trail that leads through the park. Just follow that trail, and go through a marked shallow swamp. At the other end of the swamp, you will end up on 5th Street. Follow 5th Street until you come out to Rio Drive. Once you hit Rio Drive, make a right and keep running down that road. You will see a few tall buildings way off in the distance. Head that way. You can choose to run down the beach in the sand or on the boardwalk that follows along the beach. Run until you reach the mouth of the Blue Inlet at the very end. The team bus will be waiting there to take us all back to the base."

It was summertime, humid, and hot. We all boarded the team bus, and off we went to the Lumpkin Park. When we all finished a brief moment of stretching our muscles, we commenced this idiotic run. As usual, the gazelles took off. These are the young guys fresh out of SEAL training who are in the best shape that they will ever be in in their lives. I decided to pace myself, as I was unsure of the course that I was running, and as I was from the West Coast, I felt sure that I was given directions for this run by some of the East Coast SEALs that could *not* be trusted.

Lumpkin Park was full of trees, thick underbrush, heavy humidity, and ninety-degree heat. As there was no cool breeze, perspiration was pouring out of me. Running through the shallow swampland was somewhat refreshing, but the mosquitos, deer flies, and water moccasins made it a pain in the ass—and a motivator to get the hell out of there.

When I came out of Lumpkin Park, I arrived on 5th Street. I ran down this road until I came out onto Rio Drive. As I turned onto Rio Drive, I looked off into the distance, and there I saw the tops of a couple of tall buildings, just as I was told there would be. As hot and sweaty as I was, the distance to those buildings seemed like I was running to Florida from New York! When I reached the area of beach with the boardwalk hugging one side, I could see some of the younger guys up ahead—shirtless, flexing their muscles, and scanning for all the cute babes along the beach. When you are old like me, you wear a shirt!

No one was running beside me, because if they did, I would have sucked all the air out of their lungs from breathing in and out so hard. I began to think to myself, *Why in the world would anyone* need *to run ten miles?* It seemed futile. Not to mention, we were wearing running shorts and running shoes. Some of us wore T-shirts because our six-packs were fading, unlike the gazelles' abs, but without our gear, what was the point? Then another thought struck me. If someone wanted to add sanity to this insane run, wear some combat gear. You know, combat boots, a camouflage shirt, pants, web gear (this holds your canteens of water, knife, magazines for your bullets, compass, and medical kit), and a backpack with about forty pounds inside it. After all, we are SEALs, and we train to fight. We are *not* Olympic marathon runners!

When I reached the mouth of the Blue Inlet, I was tired. I was not the last guy to finish, but just about. As we were all standing around, I got many *you-look-tired-old-man* looks from the young guys. So, I stood up on the bus for the ride back.

One of the young guys said, "Hey, Chief, you can have my seat." I looked at him and just said, "No thanks. You look

like you need it more than I do." That drew a few laughs. However, in truth, if I had sat down, I do not think that my legs would have had the strength to push my body back up.

After doing this weekly nonsense for three months, I devised a plan to rid myself of this lunacy. As there was a city bus that ran from Rio Drive to the Blue Inlet, it was a simple matter of money and timing. After running through "Hell's Theme Park," I decided that I would linger in the back of the pack of runners so no one would notice me fading away. When I reached the bus stop on Rio Drive, I got on the bus and rode it to Blue Inlet. Once I had arrived at Blue Inlet, I hung around out of sight until my normal position in the pack of runners would naturally show up, and then I would join in. Remember, "If you ain't cheatin', you ain't tryin'!"

After doing this for about a month (and enjoying it), I boarded the bus one fateful day and I found that my commanding officer was on the bus as well. We both looked at each other, I smiled that *I-am-busted* smile, and we both got off the bus right away. That day, the run was extremely far. We both finished the long, silent run together. Once we boarded the team bus at Blue Inlet, the CO said, "Chief, when we get back to the team area, I want to see you in my office."

"Yes, sir!" I replied. Though I knew my ass cheeks were about to lose some major weight today.

When I walked into my CO's office, he said, "Chief, you want to tell me why you are taking the bus when everyone else is finishing the entire run?"

Standing at attention, I responded, "Because no one else thought of it, sir."

"So, Chief, you are saying that you were showing initiative?"

"Yes, sir, that is correct, sir."

"Well, Chief, since you feel that my idea of a run is not worth your time, please tell me something. What would *you* like to do on a Friday for a workout? Play volleyball? Water polo? Or would you like to just lounge around and have a few officers rub your feet?"

Thinking to myself that last idea wasn't so bad, I instead responded with my original thought about the lunacy of this type of Friday run: "Sir, with all due respect, when is the last time that you saw anyone in combat wearing running shorts, running shoes, and no shirts? Sir, we are SEALs. I feel that the men should wear some combat gear. They should wear combat boots, camouflage shirts, pants, their web gear, and a backpack with about forty pounds inside it, and then do your run like that, which does not have to be ten miles. The four-mile run through Lumpkin Park would be enough. That is what I feel we should do for a workout on Fridays, sir. We should always be training for combat."

My CO looked at me with an evil grin and said, "Done! Tell the men that from now on, every Friday this will be what we are all going to do, and you will tell the men that it was your idea."

"Yes, sir," I said.

As he dismissed me, I thought sarcastically to myself, *He really knows how to make me popular.* I was disliked for quite a while for opening my big mouth and making a tough run even worse. But what was great about this change was that the young gazelles were no longer running way ahead of the pack, nor were they running in the soft sand along the beach to impress the babes, as there were no babes in the swamp. It was the older guys who were now finishing with them or just a few feet ahead of them! Why? Perhaps older guys know how to pace themselves when weighed down. Or, it just might be because older guys know how to cheat better than the younger guys!

At any rate, I was looked at as a real asshole for changing the Friday long run to see babes on the beach into a Friday death run through the swamp.

This anger became tangible one day when I went to put on my combat boots. I slid my feet into each of my boots, and while we were on the bus en route to Lumpkin Park to begin our combat run, my feet began to itch badly. I began to stomp my feet to try to satisfy the itching. However, nothing

I did worked, and it was getting worse. I took off my boots and shook them out, only to see a fine red dust come out of each boot. By this time my feet were painfully itching. It would seem that I was the target of an itching powder payback! The guys were all laughing as I put my boots back on, and smiling back at all of them I said, "Gentlemen, you have opened Pandora's box." It took a while, but after running through the swamp in about two feet of water, the itching finally went away. Oooooh, my feet finally felt so good!

Chapter 2

GUARD DUTY TURNED PRANK...ON ME!

Being an enlisted man in the military, we all get our fair share of standing guard duty somewhere. In the SEAL teams, we would get ours on any of the bases where we are stationed and trained. I would always look forward to the one week of camp guard duty out in the California desert where we would all go to do training.

What was the appeal? Well, it was great to get away from everything that is "official" on the West Coast, and to be on your own without anyone telling you what to do every day. In other words, no adult supervision. Camp guard duty only required that the camp was secure, maintained, and that nothing was stolen. Other than that, your time was your own!

As guard duty out in the remote desert camp would always require that there be a minimum of two SEALs guarding the camp (this was for safety, although I'm not sure whose safety they were concerned about), it would help pass the time if you were with a fellow SEAL who was a bit paranoid and believed that the "bad guys" were always coming to get him. You could have a great time messing around with a guy like that. Ross was the typical post-traumatic stress disorder (PTSD) guy that you could have a lot of fun with, and at *his* expense.

Ross would sleep with a pistol under his pillow, take a weapon in the shower with him, and hide a knife inside his refrigerator, next to the beer.

One day, while we were both out at the desert camp, Ross told me that he was taking the jeep into town to buy some food. As town was well over an hour away, I knew that he would not be back for a while; this gave me plenty of time to put into action a practical joke that I had been planning.

I pulled together a few things for my practical joke. Nothing big, just a few things like black powder for explosives, PVC pipes, radio receivers and transmitters, a shovel, and a few sandbags. I put together three explosive charges and positioned the charges just outside the main gate where all the vehicles had to be parked—and near the position where Ross would be parking the jeep, just inside the SEAL training compound.

I placed each explosive charge on the side of the parking area behind the sandbags (as this was simply a joke, and I did not want Ross to get injured). I camouflaged each position so that he would not see the location of the explosive charges. I armed all three explosive devices, then waited for Ross to return. Giggling like a kid, I couldn't help but imagine how Ross was going to react to the explosions.

Off in the distance I could hear the familiar motor coming from the military jeep that Ross was driving, and a smirk crept up my lips. As I sat in my assault position in a lounge chair with a beer cooler all nicely concealed under an ironwood tree, and more importantly, out of sight from Ross, I watched as he pulled up into the parking position for the jeep. Ross shut the engine off; he then grabbed his two grocery bags of food and started walking toward the main door entrance of the camp building. With a childish grin on my face, I set off the first explosive charge with my radio detonator, and just as Ross was trained to do, he dove down and hit the dirt. I then set off the other two explosive charges, while Ross rolled a few times and quickly crawled to cover. As he laid there in the sand looking around for an attack that would never come, he realized where he was and yelled out, "Allmon! You son of a bitch!"

I was laughing out loud at Ross' reaction to my joke, and as Ross approached me, I started to howl with laughter. Ross was covered with the stains of milk and eggs on his shirt from when he hit the dirt during the first explosion. He was clearly pissed at me, but I didn't care... it was just too funny! I ended up giving Ross money for the damaged groceries and told him that he could go back to town and buy more food. With a glare he responded, "F--k you, Allmon."

But the battle had just begun.

That night, while Ross was sleeping (I know, I am an ass), I took a grenade simulator that we use for training exercises. This equaled to a little less than a fourth a stick of dynamite, and I rigged it underneath his bed. I set the timer for about ten minutes, then I left our sleeping quarters. The anticipation of the impending explosion was becoming more than I could stand, and for a brief moment, a stupid thought passed through my mind: Should I go in there and stop the timer? Then the concern passed. Screw that! This is going to be funny! *After all, he is a friend, and a SEAL brother; he will understand the humor of this.*

I waited for the timer to count down... Ten minutes passed by, and nothing happened. No explosion. I waited for fifteen minutes... Twenty minutes... until thirty minutes had passed and still nothing. Screw it; I figured that it must have been a bad timer. I decided to change it out in the morning, and then set it to go off when Ross was in the shower.

I went back to bed, and as I rested in my bed smiling about what I was going to do to Ross in the morning and how he would react... *BOOM*! I bolted up in my bed so fast that I hit my head on the bed that was above me. I heard

Ross laughing between words as he said, "How do *you* like it, Billy?"

Great, Ross did a payback on me, and it was clear now that this was going to be a long and sleepless week of guard duty!

In the morning, while eating our breakfast, we both looked at each other, nodding our heads with that "it is on" look. Ross may have had PTSD, but he also had a devious sense of humor. We both agreed that we would only have one rule: No one gets physically hurt with any of our pranks. Fair enough.

Our days were filled with the mundane tasks of surveying the ranges, blowing up unexploded explosive charges that were lying about, and building targets that needed to be constructed for other SEAL training missions. The work was long, hot, and boring. So when we were finished, as the saying goes, "It's Miller time." Time to kick back, relax, watch a movie, or… target your SEAL brother.

Each day was filled with tension, as we both were on edge, because wherever we walked, whatever we did, whatever we picked up, whatever door we opened, whatever light switch we flipped… we never knew what might set off some sort of an explosive charge!

Now, SEALs love practical jokes as much as anyone else does—you are considered a boring person if you don't—however, when you have to be "on guard" 24/7, knowing that you are targeted for an explosive charge set to go off at any moment, well, it wears you down, big-time.

While Ross was out getting some practice in on the sniper range, I was watching *M*A*S*H* on TV, laughing at Klinger wearing a dress in a mobile army surgical hospital. It was at that moment when I thought of a devious plan to execute against Ross. Ross always enjoyed his morning bowel movements, so I thought what better position for an explosive charge than inside the false ceiling—over the toilet? So, while Ross was working on a tighter shot group on the sniper range, I carefully planted a small explosive charge in the false ceiling over the toilet in our bathroom.

The next morning, when Ross went into the bathroom, I just sat in the TV room chuckling at my ingenuity. I didn't have to wait long, for as soon as I felt Ross had checked out the area where he was going to be for the next twenty minutes, and when I felt that he was comfortable, I pushed the button on my radio-firing device... *BOOM*! Immediately following, I heard nothing. However, when Ross came out of the bathroom and walked into the TV room where I was sitting, he emerged all covered in white dust from the ceiling tiles that rained down on him. It was a great sight! I sat there with a big grin on my face and said, "Got ya!"

Ross stared at me long and hard as he nodded his head. Then without a word, he turned around and went back into the bathroom to finish his morning duty.

The next day we were both showing signs of exhaustion from lack of sleep. I was still poking around, looking everywhere for trip wires, pressure plates, radio receivers, and anything that looked like it may set off an explosive charge. I started to feel good about my detection abilities because, from time to time, I would find a pressure plate, trip wire, radio receiver, or a motion sensor, and I would disarm the device. Ross was clearly pissed off at me for finding his devices. I also made matters worse by teasing him about his sloppiness and his lack of deviant ingenuity, telling him he needed to take a refresher course on Improvised Explosive Tactics 101.

The next day we were finished with our guard duty, and we completed our "turnover of duties" to the new SEAL guards that took our places. We said good-bye to them, and I told Ross that he was a good sport. He flipped me the "bird" and sped off in his van, and I departed in my car. At Pine Valley, we stopped at a café to get a bite to eat. Ross was laughing about our practical jokes, as was I. It was good fun and it made for great memories later.

When we finished our meals, Ross and I went out to our vehicles, and we departed for San Diego. Ross' van was ahead of me, and as we were heading down the highway, we came upon a state trooper safety checkpoint. On the road I found Ross pulled over, and he was speaking with the patrol officer. After a few moments Ross proceeded without any problems. I pulled up into the center of the checkpoint; it was at that moment I heard a very loud *BOOM*!

Damn that Ross! I was dragged out of my car and handcuffed. The officers searched my car for explosives and weapons. I asked the officers what was going on. The officer that Ross had spoken with said that the driver ahead of me claimed that I was carrying explosives and weapons out in the desert (a true statement, but *not* what this state trooper was thinking). I told the officer that he and I work together, and that this was just a joke. However, the officers were not laughing. The officers informed me that they were impounding my car.

Amid the chaos, I got to talk to a lot of interesting people from the California Highway Patrol Department about the transporting of explosives and weapons. After they searched my entire car and found nothing, they questioned me further, and they also contacted my command (I took the Sergeant Schultz motto, and kept repeating, "I know nothing").

Seven hours had slowly passed before I was finally released. But only after being thoroughly probed, prodded, questioned, photographed, and forced to sign all kinds of documents to the statements that I made.

Good one, Ross! In case you're wondering, we're *not* even, although the years have passed. It is still on!

And yes, it was totally worth it.

Chapter 3

GOT SORE FEET FROM RUNNING? TRY THE CURE THAT NAVY SEALS USE

My son has a few gullible friends who buy into anything that a SEAL may talk about, which is just about everything. After all, everyone knows that SEALs have seen and done just about everything. Lord knows that some of those stories are tough to live up to! Being in the SEALs gives one an appreciation for what Davy Crockett must have had to endure when hearing the BS stories about himself regarding what he was supposed to have done in his life.

One day, while dining out with my son and a few of his friends, my son's friend Nick told me that he was going into the Navy, and that he wanted to become a SEAL. Looking at this young man, so eager to serve his country, and to do it in a profession that demands so much personal sacrifice,

I said to him, "Are you really sure that this is what you want to do?"

Nick stuck his chest out and proudly said, "Yes, sir, Mr. Allmon, I sure am!"

I could not help but smile at such patriotism. "Nick," I said, "what have you been doing to prepare yourself for a life in the SEAL teams?"

Nick looked at me with a slight grin on his face and said, "Well, I have been working out every day. I have been doing a lot of swimming in the pool at the recreation center, but I haven't been running too much, because I got bruises on the bottoms of my feet."

"Bruises?" I asked. "How the heck did you get bruises on the bottoms of your feet?"

"Not sure. I guess that my feet hit the ground too hard when I run."

"So how do you run? Do you run pounding your feet to the ground? You must look like a moron in your sleeveless shirt and tight running shorts, while stomping your feet as you go down the road."

Nick was not amused as his friends began mocking him by putting their arms up like a dog that begs, then collectively stomping their feet under the table.

Looking at his friends, Nick protested, "I do not run like that! Mr. Allmon, I guess that it is from running on the balls of my feet, and now they hurt too much for me to run on them."

Looking back, I should not have let the "balls of my feet" comment go, but what the heck—I felt that he was already being harassed enough by his peers in public.

Nick then looked at me and said, "Mr. Allmon, do you know of anything that I could do to get rid of the pain in my feet, so that I can return to running?"

I sat silent for a moment, and then I looked at Nick seriously and said, "If you are truly serious about curing the pain in your feet, you can do what the rest of the SEALs do when they have a problem like yours. It is a very old remedy that has been passed down from one SEAL to another. Nick, this cure has been around for many years, but you have to follow these instructions carefully. You need to purchase three big jars of sauerkraut; it must be jars and not cans. Empty all three jars of sauerkraut into a large pot and simmer—do not boil it—for one hour on top of your stove. Add filtered or bottled water to maintain the original fluid level in the pot. It is important that you do not add tap water; it must be filtered or bottled water. After you have simmered the sauerkraut for one hour, let it cool to 100 degrees Fahrenheit, then soak both your feet in the sauerkraut juice for thirty minutes two times a day. You must do this for two weeks nonstop. Do you understand this?"

"Yes, sir, Mr. Allmon, I totally understand. That will cure the pain in my feet?"

I nodded. "Yes it will, Nick, but only if you follow those instructions."

Every day my son would call Nick to make sure that he was soaking his feet in the simmered sauerkraut juice. To my delight, Nick was true to his word. In fact, his feet soaking got so intense that his wife asked him to soak his feet outside the house, as she could no longer tolerate the smell of boiling sauerkraut.

As it would happen, our yearly SEAL team reunion was coming up; my son invited Nick to come with him, as it was a family day. Nick was proudly telling all of my SEAL brothers about his desire to become a SEAL, and his dedication to the remedy that I had given him for his sore feet. It was great watching Nick enthusiastically explaining how he followed my instructions on how to prepare and use the sauerkraut juice for his sore feet. My SEAL brothers looked at Nick and laughed.

Finally one of my SEAL brothers said, "Nick, don't feel bad about that joke. You are not the first victim of one of Chief Allmon's pranks."

Nick was clearly shocked. "Joke? It was a joke? Oh my God, I feel like such an idiot!"

Nick stood numbly shaking his head in disbelief that he was pranked by someone that he admired and respected.

To aid his broken ego I yelled out, "Hey, Nick, I still love you!"

Upon learning what I had put her husband through, Nick's wife was not too happy with me either and said to me, "Next time, please leave me out of your damn jokes."

Sure, of course I will... not!

Chapter 4

GOT HEMORRHOIDS? TRY THIS ANCIENT CHINESE CURE

It is truly funny to me that when it comes to medical advice, people will seek out the advice of their friends instead of a doctor. When they seek me out for medical advice, I feel that it is not my fault that they are the ones who will subject themselves to my recommended treatments for whatever it is that is ailing them. Hey, I am *not* a doctor!

It is true that one does not need to run to a doctor for every little problem that a human body will have or be subjected to throughout the years. For some of these problems we can and do take the advice of our friends or loved ones—as long as the advice makes sense.

Just ask Walter about my friendly medical advice. Walter came to me, and for whatever reason, he felt the need to confide in me that he had a very bad case of hemorrhoids. I guess that he read my first book and knew that I would understand and truly care about the kind of pain that he was in, and he wanted to know what would be the best treatment for such a problem.

Looking at Walter, and knowing the kind of pain that he was in, I told him that he had two choices. "First, you can purchase a tube of Preparation H, or... if you would like to cure this problem and never have them come back again for the rest of your life, you can try the following ancient Chinese method for curing this painful problem."

Walter looked at me with hope in his eyes and said, "You mean there is an ancient cure for this, and they never come back?"

"That's right, Walter."

"Tell me the cure!"

"Well, this cure is going to sound a bit strange, but what doesn't sound strange coming from China? Remember how everyone would laugh at acupuncture? The very idea that sticking needles into various nerve points on the body to cure people of their ailments was deemed ludicrous! But now it is an accepted medical practice that helps millions of people every day."

"That is very true," said Walter. "So, I should go for acupuncture?"

"No, Walter, this cure is much simpler. However, you need to follow the instructions very carefully or the cure will not work."

Walter nodded eagerly. "I'm ready! Tell me how to get rid of these damn things."

"Okay, Walter, first you need to purchase a jar of dill pickles, but not just any jar of dill pickles. It is very important that the pickles were grown in the Imperial Valley of California, as it is along the same latitude as China. The pickles must be no thicker than your thumb, and no longer than four inches. You must empty the pickle juice from the jar and replace it with oolong tea. Let the pickles sit in that tea for twenty-four hours before you use them. Empty the jar of the oolong tea, then fill the jar with a mixture of oolong tea and virgin olive oil that has been simmered but not boiled. The pickles must sit in the jar for twenty-four hours in order to absorb the mixture."

I watched the mental checklist take place inside Walter's head as he paid close attention to my every word.

"After twenty-four hours," I continued, "before you go to bed at night, take out one of the pickles and dip it in extra virgin olive oil, then insert it inside your rectum. Leave it in there until your morning bowel movement. You must do this every night for seven days in order for the pickles to permanently cure your hemorrhoids."

"What does the oolong tea do?" asked Walter.

I explained that it acted as an anti-inflammatory when combined with the healing properties of the pickle and the virgin olive oil.

With an expectant smile, Walter said, "Wow, those Chinese sure know their stuff!"

"You got that right, Walter. It may sound weird, but it truly does work, and mine never came back after doing it."

A week later, at the end of his seventh day of "treatment," Walter called me and said that he still had the hemorrhoids, but now he was starting to find traces of blood coming out of his rectum. Feeling a tinge of guilt, I told Walter that he had better go to the emergency room and tell the doctors about the Chinese cure that he had been using so that they could better identify his problem, because it may not just be the hemorrhoids.

When Walter got to the emergency room, he told me that he had a lot of doctors and nurses come in to see him, as he explained several times the "ancient Chinese cure for hemorrhoids" that I recommended. Needless to say, Walter cursed at me over his cell phone. I wish that I could have been there!

Walter no longer seeks my medical advice, which is truly a shame, as I wanted him to try my surefire treatments for weight loss.

Chapter 5

RUNNING WITH DEVILS

During some operations, the environment that you are conducting your missions in can be more deadly than the bad guys that you are going after. SEALs pride themselves on going after bad guys anywhere, at any time of the year, and where a reasonable person would never dream of going. Because in doing so, you increase the element of surprise and the chance of completing your mission with few or no casualties to your patrol.

Such was the time when our platoon conducted a prisoner recovery mission. Although this was a training mission, like all training missions it was conducted as close to the real thing as possible. Our mission was to launch from a submarine about sixty feet below the surface, take out our rubber boat and weapons and equipment, inflate the rubber boat, and launch from twenty miles off the coast. Once we motored onto the beach, we were to bury the boat and then patrol seventy miles inland to the location of a prisoner-of-war camp, rescue a downed pilot that was being held captive there, and then patrol ten more miles to a clearing where we would set up a Fulton recovery system—a system where you attach a harness to a person, release a helium balloon on a 500-foot wire that is also attached to the person being rescued/extracted, and then a C-130 aircraft comes along to snatch the steel line, which will then haul the person up to be winched inside the aircraft. Yes, it's a crazy concept! After the pilot was recovered, we were to patrol back to the beach another seventy miles, recover our boat, and return to the submarine.

Typically, the more "support stuff" that is involved to complete your mission, the more difficult your mission becomes. Subsequently, the degree of success drops. Equipment breaks down, aircraft get re-tasked for higher priorities, or worst case, they get shot down. The multi-billion-dollar submarines and their crews are worth more than a handful of SEALs, so if there are any enemy ships, submarines, or aircraft in the area, you won't get picked up, and you will be on your own to get back home.

Some might think that the South Pacific would be a beautiful area to vacation. It may well be, but not during the typhoon season on a military mission. Our platoon was on board a submarine. We were all checking our equipment and going over our time schedules when the chief of the boat (COB) came into the forward torpedo room where we all were, and told us that the winds on the surface were gusting up to 60 mph, and the sea state was pretty rough with about fifteen-foot swells. This should have been a warning that this was going to be a ballbuster of a training mission, but what the hell—we train in the water, and the winds were blowing in our favor so that the sounds of our outboard motor would not be heard by any guards that might be near or on the beach area.

As the submarine was not going to surface, we had to "lockout" (a term that means enter a watertight chamber, flood it with seawater, open the outer watertight door, and swim to the surface with all your equipment) of the submarine. While surfacing, we were to inflate our rubber boat, with the engine attached, and swim our operational gear to the surface. Once at the surface, we would tie all the loose stuff inside our boat, start the engine, and head toward our insertion point on the enemy beach.

The surface winds felt like they were gusting 100 mph instead of 50 to 60 mph, because the rain, being blown by the wind, was stinging our faces and hands. (Those who ride motorcycles in the rain know this feeling only too well). Being out on the ocean with fifteen-foot swells, in a small rubber boat, was like enduring a perpetual roller coaster ride, and this ride was going to cover twenty miles! I cannot remember a time in our training where any instructor said anything about motoring a rubber boat in a typhoon!

When our boat bobbed at the bottom of the wave and you stared up at the top of the wave, it looked like it was up thirty feet instead of fifteen! There were times when we thought that the waves were just going to swallow us whole and take us down to the bottom of the ocean to visit with Davy Jones forever.

As we were motoring toward our insertion point, one of the guys started singing Gordon Lightfoot's song, "The Wreck of the *Edmund Fitzgerald*." Not a very comforting song, but it fit our situation perfectly, because the waves were turning minutes into hours. Because of the bad weather, by the time we reached our insertion point we were four hours behind schedule. On the beach, we found a great place to bury our boat to keep it undetected by the enemy. We all moved off the beach and into the jungle.

At this point, we all took out our gear, squad radios, high-frequency radios to talk to the submarine, and night-vision goggles. We did not use any GPS systems, as the radio signals cannot penetrate through the thick jungle growth. You have to use your maps and your compasses if you want to get to where you need to go.

Once all the gear was checked to ensure that it was functioning, we found that several of the squad radios had been flooded with saltwater, so they could not be used, and it was the same with several of the night-vision goggles. At least all of our weapons were in good working order. We located our position on the map and proceeded on with our mission.

As the winds were blowing hard and the rain from the typhoon came down heavy, we did not have to worry about being quiet, so we decided to push hard to make up for lost time on the ocean. This jungle was not the best to patrol through; it was dense with thorny vines, which tore our clothes to shreds, not to mention cut into our skin.

After six hours of patrolling, we had only covered 100 yards because of the denseness of the foliage. We decided to stop and rest for an hour. The rains had stopped, and the winds had calmed down, and soon we began hearing the familiar sounds of the jungle animals and insects returning. Hacking your way through the jungle, like in the movies, is not very tactical, and it tells everyone that idiots are approaching. We used pruning shears; they are fairly silent and faster than a machete. This jungle was so thick that if you stuck your arm out in front of you, you would not be able to see your hand.

We finally came to an area of jungle where we could all sit around and see each other. I looked over at my friend Bob, leaning against his backpack and staring straight up toward the sky. So I looked up to see what he was looking at, and I saw a small patch of blue sky through the jungle canopy.

By this time we were all gazing up at it. It was beautiful, and it was blue, wide open, and free—not green, brown, and suffocating, like where we all were.

I set up our only working high-frequency radio and made contact with the submarine. We let them know of our status and position in code; we then proceeded with our mission.

It is amazing how cold it gets in the jungle at night when you are soaking wet from the saltwater and sweat. Patrolling through this particular jungle at night is nearly impossible, so we opted to sleep at night and patrol during the daylight hours for the sake of stealth and speed. Nighttime in the jungle is really cool, with lots of noises from all kinds of insects and animals, and when they stop making their noises, it means something large is approaching... like a man, leopard, or panther. Either way, it is not a good sign! The nighttime also brings out the snakes, spiders, and scorpions, not to mention the ever-present mosquitoes.

The following morning brought a strange surprise: A tribe of monkeys moved into our area, and they were loudly complaining about our presence, so we began patrolling out of the area. The jungle was hot and humid in the daytime, and it was not long before we ran out of water. Go figure—no water after all that rain! Fortunately, we found a small pond that we patrolled up to; we would push away the surface algae to refill all of our canteens. The water was dirty, but it was liquid, and for us, that was all that mattered.

With our technique of patrolling, we had made up a lot of time; in fact, we were only forty-five minutes behind our mission schedule. While patrolling we could smell burning wood, so we halted our patrol to listen for any voices. As we eavesdropped on the voices, we knew that we were close to the prisoner-of-war camp. The voices we heard were coming from the perimeter guards.

At that point we formulated a different plan of attack. As we had no idea where the pilot was being held in the camp, we decided to eliminate one of the perimeter guards and take the other one for interrogation. We silently patrolled to where the perimeter guards were, then sent in two of our team members to complete their kill-and-capture mission, while the rest of us moved into position to provide cover fire, should they need it. Watching Paul and Jake take the guards down was very cool—a stun gun to both of them did the trick, and they marked one as dead and took the other to our position for interrogation.

As we questioned the perimeter guard about the location of the pilot, he was not going to tell us, so Paul hit him with another 80 million volts from the stun gun, which seemed to refresh his memory as he hastily told us where the pilot was being held. We then marked him as dead before patrolling out to a pre-attack point to assess what would be our best course of action to assault and rescue the pilot.

Our plan was simple: Position two snipers to eliminate any threats to the five of us going in to rescue the pilot. Once the snipers were in position, we stealthily patrolled up to a part of the perimeter fence and cut our way in. The snipers were keeping us informed about any guard movement that would pose a threat to us in our area.

Once we were all inside, we quickly moved to the position where the pilot was being held, cut the lock on the door of his hut, and did a bona fide check to ensure that he was indeed the pilot that we came for. Upon confirmation of this, we placed him in the center of our patrol and quickly moved out. Our snipers informed us that a perimeter patrol was heading in our direction about fifty yards away, so we quickly moved toward a fence where we cut a hole, then all went through it and quickly resealed it. We moved out to our rally point where the snipers were already waiting for us. It was at that time that the camp siren went off. The whole camp was coming to life and suiting up to find us.

We patrolled as quickly and as quietly as we could to the predesignated pickup point for the pilot. Once we arrived, we set up our perimeter defense and started placing the harness on the pilot. We contacted the C-130 aircraft and told him that we were ready for the pickup. Once the

C-130 was five miles out, we inflated the balloon that was attached by a steel cable to the pilot's harness and sent it 500 feet up. We could hear the enemy approaching, and we really did not want to engage them. Luckily, it was at that moment the C-130 snatched the steel cable and the pilot took off like a bat out of hell! Now that that part of our mission was complete, we stealthily patrolled out, leaving the bad guys behind.

The seventy miles that we had to patrol back to our insertion position was going to suck. After a day and a night, we arrived at the point where our rubber boat was buried. However, when we checked out the beach, we saw that it was being patrolled by bad guys and there were enemy patrol boats moving up and down the coastline. We contacted the submarine and informed them of our status and current situation. The submarine replied with bad news: It was too dangerous for them to remain on site and we should try again tomorrow at the same time. Well, no good deed goes unpunished.

We had to get away from the beach area and move to a better defendable position and wait to see if the enemy patrols would go away, or present a pattern that we could exploit. Soon we found a great place that afforded concealment, but it was only about an hour after we moved in that we found out we had a real problem. Paul was getting eaten by red ants! We turned our flashlights on him, but we could not see the buggers, because our flashlights had red lenses on them. Soon the red ants were assaulting us all. We moved away from that spot and Paul stripped his clothes off and poured a canteen of water on his skin to wash off the ants as well as shake them out of his clothes.

The timing couldn't have been worse. While we're covered in biting red ants, an enemy patrol was heading in our direction, so we had to move out to a better position. Paul, being naked, stood out like a pair of dog's balls. There was no time for Paul to put his clothes back on, so the naked warrior moved out with the rest of us. Once we were back inside the jungle, we formed a tight perimeter, dug our fighting positions, then camouflaged our positions as best as we could. Apparently our best was good enough as the enemy patrol passed us by, keeping us undetected.

Come daylight, we sent out a two-man patrol to check the beach for enemy activity—Redman (named because that was the only brand of tobacco that he would chew) and Clapman (aptly called because he caught the clap, aka gonorrhea, seven times).

After a few hours had passed, Redman and Clapman returned with their report. They informed us that there were no enemy patrols on the beach. However, there were still patrol boats going up and down the coastline. So now the plan was to contact the submarine and let them know that we were ready to move to their position and be recovered.

When dusk came, we moved out toward the position of our buried boat and motor. Our officer, nicknamed Wookie because of all the hair on his body, sent two of us to do a recon of the cliff area that overlooked the beach to search out any enemy positions that might be there. Paul, now renamed "Ant-man," and I went on our way to find any bad guys. It started to rain, which was good for us, as it covered any noise that we were making. Paul spotted what appeared to be an enemy machine gun position. So, we made the quick decision to kill them both. As the two guys were under a tarp to stay dry, the rain hitting on the tarp covered any sounds of our approach on them. It was an easy kill for us. After killing them, we tagged them as dead and took their machine gun and radio, so that we did not have to worry about someone finding them dead and replacing them with two new guys.

When we arrived back at our rally point, we gave our report to Wookie. Wookie gave the order to move out and get the rubber boat in the water. Once the boat was ready, we all climbed in, placed our weapons on the floor of the boat, and sprawled out on the large outer tube of the boat to remain non-radar detectible. We started paddling out to sea without the motor running so that no one could hear us. Once we were far enough away from the beach, we started the motor and headed out to sea, evading the enemy patrol boats with ease. This ride out to sea was a lot better than the ride in, as we were only dealing with six-foot swells instead of fifteen-foot ones.

Once we were in the perimeter of the submarine, we started to signal for the sub to pick us up by signaling the Morse code "A" with one of our red-lens flashlights. When the submarine spotted us, they replied with the Morse code letter for "C" through their periscope. The submarine hovered at our position as Clapman was securing a towrope around the periscope so the submarine could tow us further out to sea. As our luck would have it, one of the enemy patrol boats spotted us, and it began speeding toward our location while Clapman clung to the periscope. The submarine must have heard the engines from the patrol boat, because it flashed the Morse code letter for "M," which meant for us to break loose from the periscope, as they were going to go down deep!

Clapman, still hanging onto the periscope, yelled into it, "Don't leave us, you assholes!" But one submarine and its crew is worth more than any SEAL squad. So, down it went with Clapman clutching it until they both disappeared below the surface of the water. It was about a minute later when Clapman popped up to the surface cussing and mad as hell that our ride had abandoned us. The only logical thing to do was to cut huge holes in our rubber boat and let it sink so that we could make ourselves a smaller target to find on the water.

When the patrol boat arrived in our area, they turned their searchlight on and began scanning the water surface for us. When the spotlight passed near us, we would submerge under water until the light moved on. Our scheme worked, and the patrol boat moved out of our area. It seemed like hours that we were in the ocean waiting to be eaten by sharks. However, our water taxi—the submarine—did come back for us, and we were all recovered. Clapman apologized to the captain for cursing him out through the periscope, but the captain shook it off. "Don't feel bad, son. I thought you were going to hang on until we reached 200 feet before letting go, so I lost the bet with my executive officer!"

With the mission declared a success, Wookie requested a meeting with all the officers and men of the submarine at the officer's club in port. We presented them with an IBS (Inflatable Boat Small) paddle displaying a large SEAL trident on it that included a brass plaque with all of their names on it, and this inscription: "For your bravery, honor, and dedication to never leave anyone behind, the members of SEAL Team One salute you."

The CO of the sub said that he would have it mounted in the dining hall of the sub as a reminder to the entire crew of their accomplishments. But he wished that he could have had a picture of Clapman's face as he was cussing into the periscope to go with the paddle!

Chapter 6

PRANKS ON SEAL WIVES—BAD IDEA

When it comes to practical jokes on SEAL wives, you need to have a strong marriage, and a big set of balls, because they are going to get kicked up into your throat when you are done with your little prank.

Ross had his van jacked up in his driveway, and he was working underneath it. I came over to his house to give him a hand as we were going to change the timing chain on his engine. It was a hot day, and Ross' wife was thoughtful, keeping us supplied with cold beers, so she was totally blameless for all of the events that were going to transpire.

While we were both working under the van, getting covered with oil and grease, Ross decided that it would be great to play a joke on his wife. So he went into his garage and brought out a moulage kit. This is a kit that contains all kinds of very realistic fake wounds in it that squirt out fake blood. The moulage kit is used to train SEAL field medics on how to treat various bullet and knife wounds on the human body during a combat training exercise.

Ross' plan was to remove the front tire and lower the vehicle down so that the wheel mount looked like it had crushed his face and neck. I was to hit the side of the car, making a loud banging sound, and throw down the tire iron to make another loud noise, and then run to the front door to yell for his wife to come out quickly, explaining that there had been a bad accident. But the hardest part was to not let her dial 9-1-1!

We were both chuckling while we finished our beers, thinking about how Ross' wife was going to react to our prank, and then we put the whole plan into motion. Ross got into position and started pumping out the fake blood from his wound so that it pooled on the driveway where he was to be injured. It all looked very cool and realistically gross.

Now, all I needed to do was make a loud *bang* on the side of the van, and throw down the tire iron... *Clangadee clang.*

Ross began screaming as if he were in severe pain, and I ran to the front door, banging on it and yelling for his wife. Hearing my calls, Saundra came running out the door, and I pointed to where Ross was. When Saundra saw Ross under the front of the van, with all that blood pooled around him and shooting out of his neck area, she fainted! I caught her as she went down and yelled, "Shit! Ross! Your wife just fainted!"

Ross hastily crawled out from under the van and ran up to the porch where his wife had fainted, and as he tried to pick her up, Ross was yelling at her to see if she was okay. She revived just long enough to see Ross covered in blood all over his face and neck, and to see blood still squirting out of his neck. With that sight, she fainted again!

Now Ross looked at me worriedly and said, "Help me get her inside."

Eyeing Ross knowingly, I said, "No thanks, man. When she comes to and finds out that this was all a joke, I am not going to be here to get my balls kicked up into my throat by your pissed off wife. Remember, my brother, this whole prank was your idea, and it is now *your* problem. I am outta here, my brother. Good luck to you with this one!"

As I made my retreat, Ross called me a coward for not staying with him, but as they say, "Sticks and stones may break my bones, but a SEAL's wife… she will kill ya!"

Ross' wife finally recovered, and she was not a happy camper, especially after waking up from passing out on her front porch, and then being dragged into their living room with Ross dripping fake blood on the carpet. It would seem, according to Ross, that his little prank pissed her off so much that he had to sleep on the living room floor with the dog for a couple of nights, and I was ordered to stay away for a while.

Well, at least that proves one thing: No matter how big of an ass you are, your dog will always love you.

Chapter 7

THE BEGINNING OF THE BROTHERHOOD

A long time ago on a warm summer day, I was walking down Main Street in my hometown of Tonawanda, New York. I looked into the window of the Navy recruiting office and saw three members of my high school swim team standing inside, so I walked in. I asked them what they were doing, and of course they said, "We are joining the Navy."

I then asked, "What are you going to do in the Navy?"

The recruiter spoke up and said, "They are going to be Frogmen in the Underwater Demolition Teams and work with high explosives."

"That sounds cool," I said. "I want to do that too!" So, to the astonishment of my parents and a few friends, I tossed aside my full college scholarship, which I got for swimming, to Princeton University, and I enlisted in the United States Navy.

After I had completed Navy boot camp, I was sent to Jet Engine Repair School in the state of Tennessee. As you had to have a military rating/job description when you are in the Navy, working on jet engines, I thought, would be cool. However, later in my career, the only jets I saw were the ones flying over my head on their way to blow the crap out of whoever the designated bad guys were. Upon completion of jet engine "A" school at Millington, Tennessee, I departed for Coronado, California, to begin my UDT training.

When I arrived at the UDT training command/compound in Coronado, California, my class (number 58) was not to start training until the following week. After I had completed checking into the UDT training command (UDTRA), I was assigned guard duty.

The instructors told me that I was now a tadpole (the embryo of a frog/frogman), and I was to stand guard duty on the armory door until I was relieved by someone (the armory is where the instructors kept some weapons and pyrotechnics that they would use during our training), which I did.

There I was, 18 years old and standing guard duty on a locked steel door in my dress blue Navy uniform thinking about what type of training I was going to be subjected to, when out of one of the Quonset huts (a barracks for trainees) ran a trainee. An instructor spotted him, and the instructor yelled, "Freeze, you maggot!" The trainee did as the instructor requested, and stood at attention while facing the instructor who told the trainee to freeze.

I watched this instructor (who looked like the Hulk) as he walked up to the trainee, putting his face to within 6 inches of the trainee's face, and he began yelling all kinds of obscenities at the trainee for not wearing his helmet while he was outside of his training barracks.

The yelling of obscenities ended with the instructor saying, "Drop down, you dummy, and start doing pushups until 'I' get tired!" The student started counting out his pushups and after about 100 pushups, the student was starting to struggle. The instructor began to yell more obscenities at the trainee for being so appallingly weak. As I stood there guarding the steel door of the armory, I was astonished as I watched this instructor kicking the trainee in the ribs with the side of his foot.

The sight of this instructor kicking the trainee troubled me, and I thought that the instructor had obviously lost his mind. So, I left my guard post at the armory door, and went into the office where the medical corpsmen were. I said to the corpsmen, "There is an instructor outside that is kicking one of the students in his ribs."

One of the corpsmen looked at me and said, "Really? Well, we have got to see this for ourselves! Lead the way, my good little tadpole!"

Both corpsmen got up from their desks and walked back outside with me; one of the corpsmen looked at me and said, "By God, you're right, tadpole, just look at that instructor." The other corpsmen yelled out to the instructor, "Hey, Big Lou! You got a new tadpole here, and he left his guard post on the armory door just to squeal on you!"

Do you know that feeling you get when you think that you are in trouble? Well, this feeling was much worse. Now, this instructor, "Big Lou" (so named because he is 6'8" tall and 220 pounds), turned away from the trainee who was lying on the ground, and slowly walked towards me.

As Big Lou approached me, I could feel my heart pounding with fear. When Big Lou was standing inches from me, he leaned down and whispered in my face with a tone of meanness that would have scared the hell out of Satan himself. "Who the f--k do you think you are, tadpole? I am going to send you through hell on earth you little f--king, snitching, piece-of-shit, want-a-be maggot, and when I am done with your sorry little tadpole ass, you will either quit or you will DIE!"

As Big Lou turned to walk away from me, I saw the word "God" embroidered on the back of his instructor's ball cap. I thought to myself, what the hell kind of training did I volunteer for? I never knew real fear until that day, and until that day, I never imagined the physical and mental torture to which I was going to be subjected by all the instructors, and in particular, Big Lou. Big Lou was on a mission, and I was going to be his daily target of opportunity.

During our class training, Big Lou was always quick to offer up many obscene words of encouragement to me, especially while standing on my stomach as I laid on my back and did flutter kicks. I was physically exhausted and hurting. However, for me, quitting was out of the question, and if I could help it, so was dying.

Every day of our basic training, our entire training class was mentally and physically tested. Once, while our training class was on a three-mile run, Big Lou would smoke a cigar and blow the smoke from his cigar into my face as we all ran down the beach. I felt like puking my guts out from breathing in that cigar smoke, but if I did puke, I was sure that Big Lou would have made me pick it up and eat it, or he would somehow torture me with it.

Whatever Big Lou's sick mind would come up with, I knew that I would have to suffer through evil he devised to make me want to quit UDT training. Big Lou always singled me out as a "volunteer" for his sick little mind games, like the volcano. This is where all the trainees sit in a circle facing out, with me in the center. One day, before our class started our three-mile run down the beach. I was told to get wet in the surf zone, and after I was wet, I was told to dive into the center of the volcano. Big Lou would yell out, "Eruption!" and every trainee would start throwing sand over their heads to bury me in the center, after which we would all go for our run down the beach covered in sand.

The real God must have been upset at Big Lou for having his instructor hat embroidered with the name "GOD" on the back of it, and possibly (though doubtful), he felt some sympathy for me. Because as luck, or divine intervention, would have it, on my fourth week of training before "Hell Week" was to begin (this is one week of extreme physical and mental training without any sleep), Big Lou retired! I thank you God, both of you!

In truth, during my time in UDT training or BUD/S (Basic Underwater Demolition/SEAL training), our entire training class (including our officers) was always badgered, mentally and physically, by all the instructors. One comment stuck with us, and that comment was made by one of our instructors, which was, "For some of you, if you aren't cheating, you aren't trying. However, if anyone or all of your stupid cheating asses ever gets caught, you will wish that you never did cheat."

As was customary in UDT training, the instructors would form all the trainees into boat crews of seven men per boat/IBS (Inflatable Boat Small), and as a boat crew you would always carry your 260-pound rubber IBS on top of your heads, everywhere you went on land. As you can well imagine that at 260 pounds, the IBS is not a light rubber boat, and as you ran along in a group with the boat on top of your heads, the heavy rubber boat would pound your heads down into your shoulders, and it would also remove what little hair you had left on top of your heads.

On one of our weekends off, our boat crew got together and agreed that we would all cheat by making the weight of our IBS lighter. Our plan as to how we would lighten our 260-pound rubber boat was a simple one: We would use helium. We all chipped in and purchased a large tank of helium gas. We waited until dark, and while out of sight of any instructors, we filled our IBS with enough helium mixed with air so that our rubber boat did not float away, and in the event a strong breeze came up, the mixture was just heavy enough that it would stay on the ground wherever we put it.

Monday was rock portage. Not all the beaches along a coastline are made of sand; some are very rocky with cliffs. Rock portage was a training exercise where we had to paddle our rubber boats out through the surf zone, and then paddle back in through the surf zone, catch a wave in our rubber boats, ride that wave all the way onto the rocks, and then drag our boats out of the water and over the large rock boulders and keep repeating the exercise until the instructors felt that we were all doing the rock portage exercise properly.

When Monday came, the instructors told us that our class was going to conduct a rock portage exercise with our rubber boats, into and onto the rocks, which were located about a mile down the beach. Depending on the size of the waves (say 6 feet or more), this could result in the breaking of IBS paddles, arms, ankles, or legs. We lifted up our boat and put it on our heads. What a huge difference! It was so light! There was little weight at all on our heads. The instructors ordered our class to run a mile down the beach, with our IBS on our heads, to the location where we were all going to conduct the surf passage through the rocks.

As we were running down the beach, our boat crew was passing all the other boat crews with ease, primarily because we were not hindered by any weight from our rubber boat (gotta love that helium). It was hard to keep from laughing at how easy it was running with our rubber boat on top of our heads, and we were all thinking that this was almost fun.

When our boat crew arrived at the designated position near the rocks, we were ordered to put our boat down. When all the other boat crews finally arrived, the instructors told the rest of our class to keep their boats on top of their heads. Because our boat crew came in first we got a break, as the instructors said, "It pays to be a winner, people!" (Or, as in our case, a bunch of cheaters).

When the instructors had completed their long explanation about how the surf passage and rock portage maneuver was to be conducted by our training class, the instructors ordered the rest of the boat crews to put down their rubber boats. As soon as this was done, we were all told to hit the surf (get wet); we all ran into the ocean without our boats to roll around in the surf zone to get completely wet. As we were coming back out of the surf zone, and slowly making our way towards the beach, we observed one of the instructors as he walked up to our IBS and for no apparent reason, he kicked our rubber boat. When the instructor did this, our IBS went skidding across the sand for about 20 feet.

All instructors' mouths opened in total disbelief at what they had just seen (how could a 260-pound rubber boat skid 20 feet across the sand?). We watched from the surf zone as all the other instructors who were standing there looked astonished at what they had just seen. They then all turned and looked at our boat crew (all seven of us with that "oh shit, we're screwed" look on our faces).

We watched from the surf zone as all the instructors walked over to our rubber boat. One instructor bent over to pick up the front of our IBS, while the other instructor bent over to pick up the rear of the IBS. As both instructors lifted our IBS up, they both tossed what should have been a 260-pound rubber boat high into the air above their heads. With that effort, all the instructors turned their anger towards our boat crew.

While we were standing there in the surf zone, waiting for the instructors to give their next command, our officer looked at us and said, "Men, may God have mercy on us, because these instructors are not going to!"

Do you know that feeling that you get when you think that you are in trouble? Well, this feeling was much worse. All the instructors told us to come in and drop down in the pushup position, which we did. The lead instructor came over to our officer and asked him if he knew anything about the lack of weight to our boat. Our officer snapped out a reply that I thought was brilliant: "No, instructor, perhaps it is the heat from the sun that is making it so light, like hot air inside a balloon." The instructor was not amused, and the instructor told our officer that he was the one full of hot air.

Then one of the instructors told a member of our boat crew to suck some of the air out of our IBS (we knew then, that we were all totally busted). As our boat crew member did what the instructor had asked, the instructor asked our boat crew member to yell out his name, and of course out came that squeaky duck voice from inhaling helium. The instructors were totally pissed off at us, and for our punishment, they told us to fill up our IBS with sand.

For the rest of the training exercise, we had sand filled up inside of our rubber boat. Going through the surf was not too bad with all that sand as it stabilized our rubber boat and kept us from flipping over whenever a wave would hit us. The killer for us was when we had to shoulder carry our IBS back to the training area. Because of all that additional weight from the wet sand, we came in last, and because we came in last we got extra time in the surf zone, rolling in the sand on the beach, doing pushups, and as a point of total torture, we were ordered to take our boat (deflated and rolled up) through the entire obstacle course.

We never filled our IBS with helium again, and the instructors were always kicking everyone's IBS before every evolution to make sure that everyone's IBS was not filled with helium.

For everyone who goes through it, BUD/S training is both physically and mentally demanding, but thank God, we had the weekends to ourselves. Some of you older SEALs and Frogmen out there might remember back in the day (prior to 1974), if you wanted to go off any military base on "liberty" (a term meaning that you were free to leave the military base and go out into the local town) you had to have a liberty pass. If your command did not issue you one, you could not leave the military base. Being in UDT training made it even worse, because only the lead boat crew (the winners of that week's training events), would be awarded the coveted liberty passes for the weekends.

So, what were the rest of us to do if we wanted to go out on the town for a good time?

Well, getting off the military base was a simple matter. I mean, all we needed to do was to put our clothes and shoes into plastic bags, swim across the bay, get dressed, and go out into the town for a good time. The Coronado Bridge was a good rest stop before swimming on into the city of San Diego. One night, we got the idea to spray paint our class number (58) on the main concrete support of the bridge before continuing with our swim into San Diego, and a few good times.

Painting our class number on the side of the Coronado Bridge was a vain and senseless move, and it proved to be our undoing. Because when a few of us, without liberty passes, were all swimming out to our favorite main bridge support one night, we were intercepted by two instructors in a PBR (Patrol Boat River), and they illuminated our position in the water with the boat's searchlight. There we all were, illuminated like four turds in a punch bowl.

Remember that feeling you got when you thought you were in trouble? Well, this feeling was much worse. It sucks to get caught, but hey, we were trainees (tadpoles) and far from being Navy SEALs. We would learn much later in our training that you never take the same route in and out of your operational area while conducting a mission, and

NOT to mark (spray paint) your rally position for others to know where you are or have been.

The instructors told all of us to get into their boat, and of course, we all did. We were told that because we felt as if we were not getting adequate swim time during our normal training hours, they were going to help us out with our desire for more training. (Of course, this was NOT what we had in mind!)

So, off we went into the night with our instructors on the PBR. We cruised out of the San Diego bay, and out into the Pacific Ocean. The four of us were huddled in the back of the boat soaking wet with nothing on but our swim trunks and flippers. The night air was cold, and so was the water, to include the hearts of our instructors. The instructors ripped open all of our plastic bags and took out our dry clothes. They removed our wallets from our pants, and from our wallets, they took our military ID cards and all our money that we had for beer. The instructors told us that the money was payment for the extra training; they then tossed all of our clothes into the ocean.

When we got next to the jetty by North Island, we were told to swim to the Coronado Bridge where we would be picked up, and to rest assured that the instructors would be there waiting for us. They kept our military ID cards and told us that we would get them back when we all arrived at the Coronado Bridge.

We all jumped into the water by the North Island Naval Air Station jetty, and started swimming back into the San Diego bay towards the Coronado Bridge. Funny that the water felt colder now than before we got caught. The instructors were in the PBR and followed along for about the first mile, and then they sped off in their boat into the night ahead of us.

As we did not see or hear the PBR anymore, we figured that they could not see any of us either. We all decided to swim into shore and make our way around the North Island shoreline to the Coronado Bridge and then swim out to where the instructors would be in their PBR. After all, we were already in trouble, and we all thought, just how much worse could it get?

Well, that question was soon to be answered. Being the stupid tadpole trainees whom we were, we did not count on being caught by these same instructors. It seems that they had figured we would do what we were doing. So, they had the PBR beach them on the shoreline where they could wait for us to run by in the event that we would try to cheat.

As far as spotting us out there swimming in the water, the elements were in their favor. Because if we swam by, they would have seen us from the light reflecting off the water caused by the perimeter security lights on the nearby military base, and they would have followed us along the shoreline. Nevertheless, we cheated, and now we were totally screwed, and the instructors were going to show us just how screwed we were going to be.

Needless to say, our instructors were very pissed off at us. They took away all of our fins, and told us to get our asses back to our barracks training area on the base as fast as we could. When we finally got back to our base, we saw our entire training class standing there with their rubber boats on top of their heads, while the instructors were hosing them down with a fire hose.

When we announced to the instructors that we had arrived, our entire training class was dropped into the pushup position, and the instructors told our class about what we had done, and that we disregarded our punishment, which was given to us by our instructors. It was because of our lack of respect to our instructors that the rest of our training class was going to suffer dearly for what we had done.

The instructors told us to go to our barracks and put on our training uniforms and report to where the rest of our training class was standing. When we came back, our training class was still in the pushup position being hosed down by the instructors. The instructors told us to stand at attention, which we did. The instructors then informed our training class that we were special, and because we were special, we did not have to do anything except watch while the rest of our training class suffered at the hands of our instructors for what we had done.

This was a difficult thing for us to watch, and it did not sit well with us. We yelled to the instructors that it was not fair to punish our entire training class for what we had done. The instructors fired back and said that it was not right what we had done, and it was not right to disregard the punishment given to us by the instructors. So, if we did not care about the punishment that we were given by the instructors, our entire training class was to suffer for what we had done, and for the punishment that we had rejected.

We told the instructors that we would carry out our punishment if they would stop punishing our entire training class for what we had done. The instructors told us to go to hell, shut up, and that for the entire night, we were to finish watching our training class being punished for our actions, and for our total disregard of the instructors' punishment for us.

We stood there at attention watching the instructors use a fire hose to spray down our classmates as they did pushups and duck walked with the rubber boats on top of their heads. We all felt like spiders' asses (the lowest thing to the ground that actually does not touch the ground that I am aware of).

When morning finally came, our training class was dismissed, and the instructors came over to us and asked us how we felt. We all replied, "Shitty."

The lead instructor said, "Good, perhaps last night you assholes learned something about respect and honor."

We did. We learned that we should take our punishment like men, and not let others suffer through a punishment for what we are responsible for doing. The lead instructor looked hard at us and said, "If you assholes cannot embrace honor, then there will never be a place for you in the SEAL teams." He then gave us back our money that he said was payment for the extra training, turned his back on us and yelled, "Return to your class, you maggots!"

Chapter 8

WE GOT NEW GUYS CHECKING IN; GET THEM MEASURED FOR THEIR BODY BAGS!

After graduating from our BUD/S training, we all received our orders to report to our new prospective commands; mine was SEAL Team One. We were all eager to go and fight in a war, any war. After all, it's what we had trained so long and hard for, is it not? When part of our training class, 19 of us (the other members of our graduating class reported to UDT 11, 12, and 13), arrived at SEAL Team One, we all got our collective welcome aboard greetings from the Command Master Chief. The Command Master Chief of SEAL Team One was a wise man of great stature, and he was well respected by all Navy SEALs.

Because we were the "new guys," all the other SEALs with combat experience were looking down on us and making remarks like, "Stupid FNGs," "Look at them in their brand new uniforms, thinking that they are SEALs," and "Those guys are just pieces of shit." We were all standing at attention, in our brand new starched green uniforms feeling, well, "new." As we were all standing there at attention, the Command Master Chief dismissed all the other SEALs, and told us to "stand by." Once the other SEALs were dismissed, the Command Master Chief imparted several encouraging words to all of us. They were momentous and heartwarming words that made you feel like you belonged to a great family. Words like: "The commanding officer did not come out here to greet you assholes today because he would rather piss in his toilet than to waste his time speaking to you worthless F--king New Guys (FNGs). You don't know shit from lips on your asses, you're just a bunch of stupid assholes with shit for brains, nothing but worthless peons that we can't use yet. My God, what the hell is going on at the training command to produce such poor excuses for want-a-be SEALs," and so on.

You have to understand that back in the day, and in the eyes of SEAL Team One, as new guys, we *were* worthless peons until we had completed SEAL Basic Indoctrination training (SBI), and Basic Airborne (parachute training). It was ONLY after completing SBI training and airborne training that you had received enough training in order to be placed into a SEAL platoon, and then you could be deployed overseas.

After our "welcome aboard" greeting by our Command Master Chief, we were then introduced to the Chief Master at Arms. The Chief Master at Arms was responsible for assigning SEALs to their daily duty assignments within the SEAL command. As we all had to wait until training slots opened for SBI and basic airborne training, the Chief Master at Arms briefed all of us on our assigned janitorial duties. After the Chief Master at Arms had completed giving his briefing to all of us FNGs, he directed all of us to go over to the medical office to get measured for our body bags. When we all started walking over to the medical office, the Chief Master at Arms yelled out to us, "You don't want to get the wrong sizes do you? If you get the wrong size, they will have to cut off your heads, or saw off your legs to fit you inside your f--king body bags, you worthless pieces of shit." I thought to myself, nothing like giving the new guys a supportive and colorful mental picture of things yet to come.

So, we (the FNGs) all started walking toward the medical office, and once we had arrived there we told the corpsmen there that we are all here to get measured for our body bags. The corpsmen said, "OK, strip down and form a line!" Why we all had to strip down to get measured for our body bags made no sense to me, but hey, we are the FNGs, and as the Command Master Chief said, "We don't know shit from lips on our asses."

We all took off our clothes as the corpsmen had asked, and the corpsmen started measuring each of us, and he yelled out our measurements to another corpsman that was writing them down on a clipboard that he had with him.

As we were all standing there in line, naked (this was long before female support types were allowed to be assigned to the SEAL teams), things appeared to be moving along rather slowly. The corpsmen were measuring all of our arms, legs, torsos, and heads, until the operations officer came waking over to us. The operations officer cocked his head in a perplexed manner while looking at the 19 naked new guys standing in a line outside the medical office. The operations officer then went inside the medical office and asked, "What the f--k is going on here?"

The corpsmen replied, "We are measuring these FNGs for their body bags, sir."

The operations officer said, "What? That's enough screwing around with these idiots! You worthless new guys get your f--king clothes back on and finish checking in!" It would seem that when it comes to body bags, one size fits all. Even if the body bags did not fit, I am sure that there were few complaints, if any at all, about them.

After we had all completed the "checking in" process, we were all assigned to X-ray platoon. This is a platoon where they assign all the FNGs for any and all crappy jobs that are needed in and around the SEAL compound while you, as a FNG, are waiting to be assigned to Basic Airborne school and SEAL Basic Indoctrination (SBI), and finally, every new SEAL's dream of dreams, to be placed into a SEAL platoon and then to be deployed overseas.

Stan and I were assigned to clean up the SEAL team community restroom. Every day it was our job to clean the 6 mirrors, 6 sinks, 6 toilets, 6 urinals, the walls, and floors. Just the kind of job every new SEAL team member dreams about having after graduating from UDT/BUDS training, and arriving at his newly assigned command.

I mean come on, after all that basic training that we went through, you arrive at an operational SEAL command, and the only thing a new SEAL is qualified to do is to clean a restroom. Well, it is true! (At least back in the 1970s it was.) After a month of cleaning the common SEAL team restroom, I had had enough. I told Stan, who was working with me every day, that I had had enough of this crappy job. I went to the Chief Master at Arms office and said, "Chief, I am sick of the job that you gave me. I didn't go through UDT/SEAL training to clean mirrors, toilets, sinks, and urinals. I want something more than this."

The Chief Master at Arms looked at me and said, "You want something more? Well, you know what, shit for brains, I think you are right; a man with your many talents who is still shitting BUD/S chow deserves something more. Come on, follow me."

I started to feel good inside myself about what I had said to the Chief Master at Arms, and I was thinking that I should have said something sooner. I thought, finally, perhaps he will assign me to the armory to work on weapons or to the parachute loft to work on parachutes or something worthwhile, which would prepare me for combat.

As we were leaving the Chief Master at Arms' office, to my dismay, we went right back into the SEAL team community restroom. The Chief Master at Arms looked at Stan and said, "Stan, because you did not complain about your assignment like Mrs. Allmon's little boy Billy here, you are relieved! Mrs. Allmon's little boy Billy, you are now in charge of the entire restroom. How's that for something more, your highness? And your highness, should you want something even more after this, please feel free to come and see me anytime, because your needs are my top priority, and I will do whatever I can to make sure that your stay with us is better than anyone else's."

Note to self, must learn to keep my big mouth shut, and choose my words more carefully. I did that crappy job for another 30 days before being sent to SBI, and after completing jump school, I finally got into a platoon. However, to this day, I still struggle to think before I speak.

Chapter 9

A BASIC BREAKDOWN OF A SEAL PLATOON: SOME DUTIES ARE BETTER THAN OTHERS

In my day, when you were assigned to a SEAL team, and after you had acquired a few operational skills, you were placed into a platoon for advanced SEAL training, and finally, your platoon was deployed overseas. Each man has key responsibilities and duties within your operational platoon. Deploying overseas is always exciting; it gives you a chance to come together as a platoon, and to deepen your bond with your SEAL teammates.

During my time in the teams, at a minimum, every SEAL platoon would have two officers. These officers are the poor brave souls that are responsible for every one of us and tasked with leading all of us on our assigned missions to hunt down and destroy the bad guys. When we all were not on a mission, it would seem that they are tasked with protecting and defending our sorry enlisted asses whenever we got into trouble.

There was one all knowing and wise chief petty officer whose duties included, but were not limited to, advising and looking out for the platoon officers, the enlisted men, and at times when a few enlisted men would get out of control, the chief petty officer would try and prevent the platoon officers from choking their enlisted men out. Depending on the personalities of the platoon, the chief might also serve as an intermediary between platoon members, and if needed, as a disciplinarian.

Two radiomen have the duties of maintaining all the electronic and radio equipment assigned to the platoon, insuring that the platoon can communicate with the rest of the world while out on a mission. God help the radioman if he cannot make communications with the SEAL platoon's support elements. Because there is nothing more threatening than an armed SEAL platoon looking at you, the radioman, when they all need to get the hell out of a hot area.

There are a few designated machine gunners strategically positioned within the SEAL platoon. These machine gunners are responsible for the total destruction of all enemy forces, and to provide cover fire for the SEAL platoon, allowing them to run like hell should the SEAL platoon be engaged by a battalion, or any force with superior numbers and firepower.

Last, but never least, is the platoon corpsman. His duties include giving us all sorts of shots, meds, killing the enemy, and stitching up our wounded asses, all at the same time.

There are other duties, responsibilities, and assignments within a SEAL platoon, but the aforementioned are pretty much the essence of an old SEAL platoon.

It is not often that you envy the abilities of another person in your platoon, as you are all valued for your professional abilities and the schools or advanced training that each of you has gone through. Nevertheless, Doc Oscar was one man that our entire SEAL platoon envied.

"Doc" is the term of endearment given to any platoon corpsman or medical person in a SEAL platoon; these corpsmen are extremely well trained in emergency field medicine for combat. However, Doc (as good as he is) is NOT a doctor.

As an operational SEAL platoon, we were all stationed together in a foreign country. During our time off, a lot of us went into the local town to mingle with the flavor of the week (or night, depending on your hunger). Our Doc, however, took an entirely different, yet professional, approach to his allotted time off.

Being a bit of an entrepreneur, Doc Oscar established himself as a local gynecologist. Doc went into all the bars and hotels that were outside the gates of our base (of which there were hundreds) and gave a quick blurb about who he was (a gynecologist) to the head madam, and offered his "services" to the "ladies of the night." Doc even had business cards printed up in town (where they would professionally print up anything you wanted).

50 % OFF YOUR FIRST TWO VISITS

Dr. J. Oscar - Obstetrics & Gynecology

I will handle your problem areas with care and compassion.

Hours of operation – 11 am – 1300 and 1700 – 1900 daily

Location – 2nd floor barracks 24B room 213

50 % OFF YOUR FIRST TWO VISITS

Doc would hand these fake business cards out to the managers and owners of all the local establishments where the ladies of the night would be working. His business cards offered 50% off their first two gynecologist visits! I ask you, the reader, is this idea pure genius or what?

Not only were these ladies of the night beating a path to his barracks' room (and that should have been a clue that he was not a real doctor. However, there is no reasoning with a woman when it comes to a sale), but they were paying him! In truth, Doc was doing everyone a service of sorts; our thoughtful corpsman did give these women shots for syphilis or pills for gonorrhea, so in that regard, he was helping these ladies of the night, and their prospective customers.

When these ladies of the night would set up an appointment to visit our Doc, he would welcome them into his room, and after a quick exam, he would respond with, "OK everything looks great," or (if they were infected) he would tell them, "I want you to take these pills and see me next week." Doc's treatment of these ladies of the night must have been really good, because he never got any complaints, and they would always come back!

I once asked Doc about his examination procedures for the ladies, and he told me that his examination process for these ladies of the night was hilarious. Doc looked at me, grinning, and said, "It goes something like this, 'Come on in and step on the scale, let me take your temperature and blood pressure.' And after I did that I asked them to pee in this fruit jar."

"Fruit jar?" I asked.

Doc said, "Yeah, fruit jar. Don't interrupt.

"After all of that, I would interview them like this, 'OK, I have a few questions to ask so please answer truthfully to the following yes or no questions, Are you having sex? Do you practice safe sex? Do you think about sex? Do you prefer one location to another? Do you accept money for sex? Do you wash after having sex? Do you perform oral sex?'"

Doc would ask other questions that were not relevant (well, not relevant from a true doctor's point of view) such as, "Did you have sex before you came to my office? How often are you having sex? How many partners do you have sex with each day? On an average, how many partners do you have sex with each week? Do you prefer to have sex in the morning, afternoon, or evening? Do you have sex with women? Do you have sex with animals?"

I am reasonably sure those are not the types of questions that a real gynecologist would ask. However, I was a radioman in a SEAL platoon, and as I am not a female, what the hell would I know about it?

Doc would also have them strip completely naked, and he would give them a full physical exam. Doc was so busy with these ladies of the night that he was booked every day of the week, and he was getting referral service too!

Whenever we were tasked with a mission that was going to take us out of the area for a while, Doc would let all the ladies of the night know that he was going to a conference in Geneva or some other medical event, and these women would have to reschedule their appointments with him so that when he came back, they could continue their visits. Doc made good money from his practice, and from time to time, he would treat us all to drinks and dinners from his profits.

The best part of all this (for Doc anyway) was that when they could not afford to pay him for their medical visit, they gave him sex as a form of payment! Again, I ask you, the reader, is this brilliance or what? Doc Oscar's whole gynecologist plan was (for Doc anyway) one of the most well thought out plans ever!

Oh yeah, for the all women reading this – Doc was a real jerk! Imagine his nerve, taking advantage of those poor prostitutes. Where were his morals? I mean really, shame on him!

Chapter 10

THINK THAT YOU MIGHT BE GOING BALD? WELL, IF YOU ARE IN A SEAL PLATOON, YOU ARE!

In the SEAL teams, it is a fact of life that the longer you serve in the SEAL teams, the more deployments you will make, and the more time you will spend with your teammates overseas on missions, training, or attending special schools. In fact, you will spend more time with your teammates than with your girlfriends or your spouses, and you will get to know your teammates' deepest thoughts and concerns.

Every SEAL platoon has at least one guy who makes you say, "Hmmm, how did he get here?" While this might be the case for a few SEAL team members who are assigned to a SEAL platoon, I know that there are several, and more serious weirdo types in civilian life, and they do not make you say hmmm, they make you say, "Damn, WHY is he here?"

Our SEAL squad was assigned as a mobile training team in a country somewhere in beautiful Central America where we were training commandos. As a few of us volunteered to extend our deployment time for an additional year, to continue training the commandos for combat, we welcomed a brand new SEAL team member named "Zack," who was assigned to our training team to assist us in the training of the commandos. Zack was a bit of an odd fellow and he was starting to go bald. Zack was extremely upset about the prospect that he was going to lose all of his hair, and he was always complaining to us that he was too young to lose his hair. (Really, I do not get what the big deal is about losing all of your hair. Does it change who you are? Are you less of a man because you do not have any hair on top of your head?)

To prevent the loss of all of his hair, Zack decided to purchase four bottles of hair grow tonic. Have you EVER known anyone (not an actor) that said, "Hey, this hair grow tonic really works!"

I would tell Zack, "You know Zack, when the enemy is shooting at you, I don't think that they really care if you have any hair or not." Zack would just raise his middle finger in response to my statement.

The instructions on the bottles of the hair grow shampoo, which Zack had purchased, instructed the user to apply the hair grow shampoo at least twice a day. Before going to sleep at night, the user was also to massage a small dab of this shampoo into their scalp, and leave it overnight until the next day when the user took their morning shower, and they could then rinse it out.

As I was thinking about how vain Zack was, and all that hair grow tonic he had purchased, I thought to myself that Zack's situation would be an excellent stress reliever for a few of us who were dealing with the occasional loss of life from the daily combat on the side of the commandos that we were all training, and it would be a great opportunity to have some fun, at Zack's expense. To cover my actions, I told everyone that I had a meeting up at the command post. I went into town and purchased a couple of bottles of the hair remover. The next day, while Zack was out training the commandos, I filled Zacks' hair grow tonic with the bottles of the hair remover I had purchased (oh come on, this is funny). I shook the bottles of hair grow tonic to ensure that my secret sauce was mixed thoroughly. I told a few of the guys about my plan so that they could share in the enjoyment of this prank of mine. After all, no practical joke is worth playing, unless it is played well and totally enjoyed by all!

The next morning, Zack came into my room all upset; he stood there in my room with his hands full of his hair and said, "Look, I am losing all of my hair! I don't know what's happening to me! What the hell could be causing this to happen!?!"

I was thinking to myself, "Yes, what indeed!" Looking at all that hair in his hands, I also thought, "Now that's a lot of damn hair! Man, that Nair stuff really works better than I thought it would."

Feeling bad for Zack (well, not really) I said, "You know what I think is causing you to lose that much hair, Zack? It is your nerves. You need to go see the doctor and ask him for some tranquilizers to help you get a nice, deep, and relaxing sleep at night. I am sure that will help you to stop losing all of your hair."

Zack looked at me and said, "Really? I think you might be right! I will go see the doctor right after I eat my breakfast."

Feeling that there was a good chance that I could be busted for my joke if Zack saw the doctor before I did, I lied to Zack and said, "Zack, I will see you later, I got a meeting right now with the base commander about some training issues that I really need to brief him on. So I'll catch up with you in a few."

I took off as fast as I could to go see our doctor before Zack did. I needed to tell the doctor what I had done before Zack came in there to see him. When I walked into the doctor's office, I told the doctor that I had a "special problem" that I needed him to keep quiet about. In fact, I said, "I want your word that you will not repeat what I am going to tell you to anyone!"

The doctor looked at me and said, "You're not pregnant are you?"

"Very funny," I said. "Now give me your word, because I do not have much time, and I really need to tell you what I have done."

The doctor gave me his word, and I proceeded to tell the doctor what I had done to Zack. We both had a good laugh about the whole thing, and the doctor told me that he would give Zack some placebos to take every night for his "nerves." To my amazement (and amusement), Zack kept using the "hair grow tonic," with my secret sauce in it. By the time he was on his second bottle of hair grow tonic, Zack had lost all of his hair.

The house cleaners whom we hired to come into our compound to do the daily washing, laundry, and room cleaning refused to go into Zack's room to clean it or to even touch any of his clothes. With all his hair falling off his head, the house cleaners felt that he had contracted some sort of contagious disease. So, every day Zack had to clean his own room, and he had to wash his own laundry.

I never told Zack what I had done to him, as I saw no logic in being shot over the loss of his hair. Besides, I felt that his newfound and permanent baldness was an improvement.

Hey Zack, if you are reading this, it was a joke! OK? Are we cool? Are you still bald?

Chapter 11

THE NAKED WARRIOR

Some SEALs, and Special Operations types, are over the top when it comes to being paranoid about the bad guys coming after them. I have known a few SEALs that had pistols under their pillows, in their shower, in their refrigerator, and in their cars. Some of these guys would "clank" when they walked with all the guns, knives, and throwing stars that they would carry on themselves to protect themselves from any would-be bad guy.

I have always felt that in combat, if it is your time to go, there is not too much that you can do to prevent it, because a well placed bullet or explosive charge could care less about all the special or advanced training that you may have had or gone through. I have known some very well-trained people who were killed by lesser-trained people. It is always sad to lose a brother, but the way many of us who live by the sword try to look at it is that it was just their time.

When a small group of us were deployed to a hostile area, we had a team house (a team house is a place where we would sleep and eat together at the end of every day) that was well fortified with individual fighting positions on the perimeter and inside our courtyard area. If we were ever attacked, we could retreat from our primary fighting positions to several fighting pits. In the event of a large-scale enemy attack, these fighting positions were to be our last stand positions where we would make the enemy pay dearly for their assault on us. If it looked like we were going to lose, we would then all escape through a thirty-two inch wide sewer drainage pipe that went from our team house area underground, to where it emptied our daily sewage, 500 feet out into the bay.

One day, I went into Marty's room, and I asked him what he was doing with all the sandbags inside his room. Marty looked at me and said that he was building a bunker. Marty, who was a young SEAL and a member of our Mobile Training Team (MTT), said that if we were ever under an enemy attack, not to run by his window where he was building his bunker. Looking at Marty, I asked him, "Why not?"

Marty said, "I might shoot you!" Marty further informed me that should we come under an enemy attack at night, that he was going to shoot anything that moved past his window. This meant me, as I had to run past his window from my room in order to get to my designated fighting position.

I looked at Marty, as if he had lost his mind, and I said, "Are you serious?"

Marty said, "Well, no. Even so, remember that I warned you, just in case you get shot." As there was no other exit for me except to run past Marty's window to get to my fighting position, and I did not know if Marty was serious or not, I got the idea to test Marty's totally absurd statement (my other idea was to throw a grenade through his window; lucky for him, I went with the following).

On a weekend that we were not too busy with the daily training of the commandos, I went into our team room (an area where we would relax and listen to a few tunes, watch the local TV, or play a movie over a few beers). I took a speaker out of our stereo system, and with about 80 feet of speaker wire, I climbed on top of our team house roof. I removed a couple of the Spanish style stone shingles to make sure that I was right above Marty's bed. Seeing that I had the correct position, I replaced the roof tiles. I placed the speaker on top of the roof tiles above Marty's bed, and I covered it with a few palm branches. I then ran the speaker wires back down to the stereo tape player that was inside our team room.

When all of my manual labor "pre-staging" work had been completed, I invited a few commandos that we had been working with to play the parts of the bad guys. We made a tape recording, which sounded something like this (only in Spanish): "Help me up.... OK, I'm up, now throw up the explosives... OK, wait here, and I will lower down the rope for the rest of us to climb up after the bomb explodes. Let me find where the stupid gringo is. I see the stupid gringo, and he is sleeping... OK, I am arming the explosives. Death to all gringos! HA HA! OK, let's get out of here... quickly... quickly before the bomb explodes... DIE, GRINGO, DIE!"

With that recording completed, and the speaker in place on top of Marty's roof, I was ready for the next phase of my operation. I informed the base guards about what I was going to do, and at the designated time that I was going to play the tape, so if they heard anything, like yelling or screaming, they should ignore it. The guards thought that I was crazy, but they liked the joke that I was going to play on Marty. I told the guards not to run into our courtyard no matter what they heard, unless they first spoke with me out in front of our iron gate, and they all agreed with me on this. I was glad that they agreed with me, because I was not sure what Marty would do when I played the tape.

After I was assured that the base guards would not react, I briefed the other MTT guys, including the base commander, on what Marty had told me about shooting anything that moved in front of his window. I also told them the reason for my joke, and that I was planning to test his statement tonight at one o'clock in the morning, to see if he was indeed serious about shooting anyone that moved past his window.

After my briefing, I invited all of them, including the commando personnel that helped to make the tape, into our team room. That night, when we were all safely inside the team room where I had the tape recorder, I told all of them that no one was to leave once I started playing the tape, to which everyone agreed.

At one in the morning, while we were all drinking a few beers, I started to play the tape. We were all giggling like a bunch of school kids at what we were hearing. When we all heard the part on the audiotape, "Die, gringo, die," the night erupted with the sound of a submachine gun being fired (thank God, I told the guards about my joke), followed by Marty screaming, "They're coming over my roof!" This was followed by more submachine gun fire. Then, everything got very quiet, and none of us dared to go outside the door, as we did not want to be shot by Marty.

A few more moments passed; we all waited and watched as our team room door slowly opened. There standing in the dim moonlit night was a naked man, holding an Uzi submachine gun in one hand, and a grenade in the other. What a sight! We all burst out laughing, that is, all of us except the naked warrior. Marty stood there looking pissed off about my joke. He called me a f--king asshole, and returned to his room with the big hole that he put in his Spanish roof tiles above his bed where he had emptied two magazines of about 60 bullets. I told Marty that he might want to rethink his bunker in the room plan, as I had a lot more jokes like this one planned for him, if he did not.

On the positive side, Marty now had a great view of all the stars through that hole in his roof. Well, that is except when it was raining.

Chapter 12

ADAPT, OVERCOME, AND IMPROVISE

At Camp Pendleton in California, there is a large military base where thousands of Marines are stationed. Our platoon was sent there to participate in a few war games against various units of the U.S. Marines. Our platoon was tasked with playing the role of the bad guys. The Marines were always happy to have us go against them. As one Marine Major put it, "If my men can prevent a SEAL element or platoon from achieving their objective, then my men can beat any enemy unit out there." It was flattering to hear, but it also creates a very competitive spirit between both the U.S. Marines and U.S. Navy SEALs, and sometimes it can get personal.

No one ever wants to fail a mission (training or real), so when we simulated blowing up a large electric power sub station that was defended by 25 Marines, the Marines said that we never made it into our target to blow it up. The Marines stated to the referee that they never saw or heard any of us, and there were no shots fired. Our officer was pissed off at this statement and said that we had indeed hit our target, and that we could prove it. The Marine referee told our officer to produce his proof, and our officer went to the electric power sub station in the daylight with the referee. When they all arrived at the power substation, our officer showed the Marine referee two timing clocks that were attached to fake explosive charges, which were mounted on the oil tanks of two very large electric power transformers.

When the Marine referee saw where the explosive charges had been placed, the Marine referee was amazed and said that we were fools to risk our lives placing the fake charges where we had because we could have been electrocuted. Our officer said, "We will do anything to accomplish our mission, but we would never say that we did something which we had not!" The Marine referee gave us the win, and the Marines who were defending the electric power sub station also showed that they were men of honor, as they had not seen or heard us; they apologized to us for their false accusation and shook our hands for a well-executed mission. We all smiled and our officer said that the reason we placed our fake explosive charges where we had was because of the tight security the Marines had around the electric power sub station, and that was the only place where we could get in. We were hoping not to be electrocuted in the process, as it was a very dangerous path to travel in order to place the fake explosive charges.

It was after that mission that a few of us decided to take a break and go into town to drink a few beers, and check out the local attractions. (Navy guys in a Marine town, what were we thinking?)

We went into a local bar and sat down for a few brews. Three girls came in that caught our attention (actually, anything female would catch our attention). We invited them over to our table to join us for a few drinks. We were all having a great time until in came several members of the U.S. Marine Corps. When they asked us where we were from (as our hair was longer than a Marine's haircut), we said the Navy. This got us the usual chuckles and the snide "Swabby" and "Squiddly Diddly" remarks.

One of the Marines walked up to our table and informed us that this was a Marine bar, open to only men. "You Navy ladies will have to leave, and these sweet ladies sitting here with you, they will be joining us men."

As you can imagine our blood began to boil a bit. As four SEALs against seventeen Marines is not the ideal win ratio, and it takes a lot to keep from fighting when you are being challenged, because numbers mean nothing to a SEAL when he is challenged, as most SEALs figure, even if a SEAL should lose the fight, the aggressors will not be bragging about it.

However, before there was any exchange of fists, our platoon corpsman (Chuck) spoke up, saying, "Gentlemen, how about letting me act as your waitress tonight? I will serve you 'men' free beers on us if you let us stay here and drink."

To which the Marines replied, "That sounds great, sweetheart!" The ladies who were sitting with us got up and left with the Marines, and we all sat back down. Chuck gave us a wink, and then he went up to the bar and ordered four pitchers of beer for the Marines.

While Chuck was at the bar, we watched him as he removed a small brown bottle that he took from his pocket, and he poured a small amount of liquid from the bottle into each pitcher of beer. Chuck then returned that small brown bottle back to his pocket. Chuck delivered the pitchers of beer to the tables of the waiting Marines, and to the women who were once sitting with us. The Marines thanked him for the beers, and for being so sweet. After dropping off their beers, Chuck rejoined us at our table.

Once we were all again sitting together, I asked Chuck what it was that he had poured into their pitchers of beer. Chuck looked at me, grinning, and said, "Ipecac." (Ipecac is a colorless vomit inducing liquid.) Chuck said, "Just sit back and wait a few minutes for the drug to take effect." After about 10 minutes, we all bore witness to the funniest and most impressive puke festival on the planet. Marines were projectile vomiting all over the place. The Marines were puking on the floor, on the tables, on each other, and they were also puking on the women that left us for the Marines! It was by far the funniest sight that we all had ever seen. As all the Marines were displaying their manhood to the ladies, we got up from our table and left them all puking. Poor bartender sure had a big mess to clean up.

So remember, guys, when you are outnumbered, take a page from the Marines and adapt, overcome, and improvise — use ipecac. Semper Fidelis!

Chapter 13

STEALTH VEHICLE

Whoever said, "Necessity is the mother of all inventions," was never a U.S. Navy SEAL. I say this because, in the SEAL teams, "Boredom is the mother of all inventions and the necessity for a well-played practical joke." When Steve and I were assigned as camp guards for one week out at the SEAL team training camp in the California desert (for you SEALs out there that know me - yeah I know, what were "they" thinking, leaving the two of us alone with our imaginations, out in the middle of the desert without adult supervision), we had to do something to keep ourselves entertained, besides guarding the camp all day, shooting bats with our shotguns at night and watching them spinning to the ground like a helicopter after it had been shot.

You have to understand that being a camp guard out in the middle of the desert is a monotonous and mind-numbing assignment. So one day, while Steve and I were sitting around drinking a few beers, we came up with the idea to affix two jeep headlights to a steel pole with wire cables that went to our jeep battery. When we would activate the on-off switch on the pole, the pole mounted jeep lights would come on. This was a true masterpiece!

Satisfied about the workings of our new invention for a joke, we sat around and waited until dark. As soon as it got dark, we locked up the entire camp and set all the alarms. We then loaded up our jeep with our "light pole" and began driving down a long flat desert highway in southern California. It was a beautiful warm starry night, but there was no traffic to be seen. We were both beginning to wonder if we were ever going to use our new invention.

As we continued driving down this long stretch of a road in our military jeep, we finally saw the lights of an oncoming vehicle way off in the distance. My partner in crime jumped into the back seat of the jeep and waited for the right moment to turn on our pole mounted jeep lights. As the oncoming vehicle got within the proper range, Steve turned on the pole mounted lights and slowly swung the light pole out to the driver's side of our jeep. From a distance, and at night, it looked like another vehicle was trying to pass us.

As the oncoming vehicle got closer, the oncoming vehicle started to flash his headlights at our phantom vehicle to warn it that he was in danger of a head-on collision. Steve waited until the vehicle was about 100 yards away, and shut off the jeep lights on the pole, and then he climbed back into the passenger seat of our jeep.

To the driver of the oncoming vehicle, it must have appeared that our "phantom vehicle" was still in the outside passing lane and coming straight at him, because the oncoming vehicle slowed to a stop, and pulled off on the side of the road. When we passed the oncoming vehicle, Steve and I looked at each other and uttered the words, "Shit, a state trooper."

I guess the state trooper was still waiting for the other vehicle that turned off its lights, because he never came after us. We put our jeep in four-wheel drive, shut off our headlights, and headed off-road out into the desert, and to a place where we felt secure that the state trooper could not see us.

As we watched from a distance, we saw that there were now two state troopers, and they were both using their searchlights to scan the entire area of the road where we had turned off our pole lights. They were scanning with their searchlights for the vehicle that had shut off its lights.

I guess they were looking for any signs of that stealth vehicle. It was funny, but we never did that again.

Chapter 14

BROKEN DICK

On some SEAL deployments, for whatever the reasons, the deployment can be more physically demanding on a platoon than on other deployments. During our SEAL platoon deployment to the Western Pacific, several members of our SEAL platoon, including myself, were beleaguered by numerous random accidents. These "accidents" took place on operational missions and exercises. The injuries were comprised of dislocated shoulders from conducting "drop and pickup." Drop and pickup is a maneuver where you would roll off a rubber boat that is tied to the side of a patrol boat at designated intervals into the water at a high speed. Once in the water, you would then swim into the shore to gather intelligence on the surface and subsurface about what is near or on the beach, and then swim back out to sea to get picked up by the same patrol boat.

When the patrol boat approached you on the surface of the water, you would be snatched out of the water by a guy inside a small rubber boat that is attached to the side of the patrol boat, and he would be holding a garden hose with a nylon rope through it. This garden hose was called a sling because it was in the shape of a sling/loop, and the guy with the sling would snag your arm, that you were holding above your head, with the sling, and pull you out of the water and back into the small rubber boat. This tactical maneuver for inserting combat swimmers works very well. However, if the boat is traveling at high speed, it will dislocate your shoulder when your arm is snagged by the sling.

There were many broken ribs from rock climbing, broken arms and legs from parachuting into the trees (not by choice), and head injuries sustained from falling off the sides of a ship at night that we had to climb up (hitting a steel deck with your head is never a good idea). All the various missions and training exercises that we had conducted throughout our entire deployment had left scars on many of us, not to mention the invisible emotional scars.

Near the end of our tour of duty, and as was customary at the time, we all had a platoon photograph taken. One photo was taken for ourselves, where we were fully suited up for combat (so cool), and one taken that was to be displayed on the quarterdeck of the command where we had served our tour of duty. The photograph that we were going to present to our unit commander was to reflect all of our injuries that we had acquired during our deployment while assigned to his command.

In preparation for this particular platoon photo, we all went over to the base medical clinic and had plaster casts put on all the various parts of our bodies, as well as bloody bandages to resemble all of our other sustained injuries. When we were all done getting bandaged up, we looked like we had just escaped from a field medical hospital in a combat zone.

The best reflection of an injury was made for Tommy. Tommy came out of the base clinic with a cast on his dick. (When Tommy was rappelling down the side of a cliff, he accidentally came down on one of the many tree branches that were protruding out of the cliff, and it stabbed his penis.) The cast was in the shape of a horizontal "L" about 18 inches long (his dream, not ours) with the short end of the "L" facing down. Tommy had a supporting wrap attached to it that went around his broken dick, and around the back of his neck to help support the cast in its horizontal broken dick position.

When Tommy walked out of the medical clinic to join us for the platoon photo, a female lieutenant walked by and said, "Oh my God, you broke your penis?"

Tommy, seeing the female lieutenant, snapped to attention and rendered the female lieutenant a hand salute, which she returned (ahh, military protocol). Looking at the female lieutenant, Tommy said, "Yes Ma'am, but it only hurts when it gets hard and starts throbbing." The female lieutenant turned beet red. Shaking her head, she turned away from Tommy and entered the medical clinic.

Tommy looked at all of us and said, "That was a stupid thing for me to say! I should have asked her for some physical therapy!" We all laughed, and then we headed off to get our platoon photograph taken. When we presented the photo of us all in plaster casts and bandaged up, the commander loved it, and said that he was going to keep this one on display in his office, and when it came time for him to transfer, he was going to take it with him.

It was a great photo, and in retrospect we all wished that we had kept a copy!

Chapter 15

WHERE IS THE GROOM?

Should a Navy SEAL ever want to keep from getting hazed by his SEAL brothers, then there are two bits of personal information that every U.S. Navy SEAL will always try to keep from his fellow teammates, and they are: his birthday, and the day that he is going to get married.

Our platoon discovered that Sam was getting married to his beautiful fiancée, and that her entire family was flying in from Texas for the big event at a Catholic church in San Diego. Before Sam was to get married to his lovely fiancée, on the eve of their wedding day, and against the wishes of his fiancée, our platoon had to have a bachelor party for Sam. Because Sam's bride-to-be protested so strongly to all of us about giving Sam a bachelor party, this was certainly going to be a great party.

Our entire platoon chipped in and rented a whole bar in downtown San Diego. We did this so that no one else could enter our little party, except for any of our other brother SEALs. It all started innocently enough, as most bachelor parties do, with plenty of drinks, girls, and so on. I think that it was about 11:00 p.m. (with all the booze we drank, who can be sure?); we were all so inebriated that we (certainly not the groom to be) had a great idea for one heck of a joke! We all took Sam to Lindbergh Field (San Diego International Airport. Of course, this was all long before 9-11 and the TSA Nazis).

We all walked up to the airline counter, supporting Sam in his drunken stupor, and purchased a one-way ticket for Sam to Boulder, Colorado. By now, Sam had passed out from all the alcohol that he had ingested. So we took his wallet, including any change that he had, and we told the stewardess that Sam was getting married tomorrow in Boulder, Colorado, and because we had his bachelor party here, could she please make sure that he got off the plane in Boulder. She smiled, and said that Sam was lucky to have such good friends like us, and she reassured us that she would make sure that Sam got off the plane in Boulder, Colorado. We thanked her, and we all left Sam to his fate.

It was around noontime, on the day that Sam and his bride to be were to be married. We were all sitting together in the church in San Diego, waiting to see Sam get married. As we (the innocent) sat there, we were all looking around for Sam. However, Sam was nowhere to be found. Sam's father walked up to us and asked us if we had seen him, and we all replied, "Not since last night, sir."

Sam's father said, "I wonder where he could be."

Yes indeed, where could Sam be, as we (now, the guilty) all started looking at each other as if we were innocent of any wrongdoing whatsoever, whispering, "Where the hell is Sam?"

As time went on, it became very clear to us that Sam was not going to make it to his wedding. So, we (the not so innocent) got up to go inside the side waiting room of the church, where the bride and all the bridesmaids were waiting to come out, to see Sam's beautiful bride, and explain to her what we thought would be taken as a funny joke.

Nothing could have been further from the truth. After explaining what we all had done to Sam, we watched as what was once a beautiful woman, turned into an ugly, venomous monster, snorting fire from her nostrils right before our eyes!

When the look of shock had left her face, and the enormity of what we had done had set in, she started cursing at us loudly (mind you, this was inside a Catholic church, and everyone could hear a pin drop), and she began slapping each of us on our faces. While we (the very guilty) were standing there taking in all of her venomous anger, in walks the priest, and all of the in-laws, to see what all the yelling and cursing was about, and why the lovely bride was so upset/pissed off.

I am here to tell you that whoever said, "Confession is good for the soul" was never a Navy SEAL at a wedding and inside a church with an angry bride ready to do battle against him.

Of course, all the in-laws were astonished when they learned what we had done to Sam. The mother of the bride was furious and said that we were the ugliest people that she had ever met in her life, and then she began to curse us (like mother, like daughter we thought). As all the women were trying to console the bride, Sam's father, who was a retired Marine colonel, walked up to us with that "you guys are so screwed smile," and in a low voice he said, "Boys, that was a good joke, but knowing how angry these ladies can get, I am sure glad that I am not any of you gentlemen." Sam's wife-to-be and her mother clearly hated all of us for ruining what they claimed to be "their wedding day." Why is it that a woman always says it is "their" or "my" wedding day? What happened to "our" (as in bride and groom) wedding day? Even so, none of us were not going to throw gasoline on that fire.

Meanwhile, back in Boulder, Colorado, Sam finally found someone that gave him enough money to make a long distance phone call to the church in San Diego, to let us all know that he was all right. We paid for Sam's flight back to San Diego, and when we all got together (and away from Sam's future wife), Sam told us that he thought our joke was funny. However, his wife-to-be told him that we were not to be invited back to the wedding the next day, nor would we be welcome in their house for any dinners for the rest of our lives. (Did she actually believe that we would trust her to cook food for us?)

We all wished Sam well, and we could not resist one last joke. While Sam and his bride were inside the church getting married, we (the forever banned) rubbed Limburger cheese all over Sam's car engine, and taped inflated condoms all over his car. We were all sure that after everything we had done, Sam's wife would never forget "her" wedding day!

Chapter 16

PAYBACK FOR FLYING FIRST CLASS

Now, do not get me wrong here, I have had my fair share of flying first class like most people have, and yes, it is nice on long trips. However, for those self-appointed "elite snobs" out there that fly ONLY first class, do not look at the rest of us boarding the plane as if we are the underlings while sipping on your mixed drink with its cute little umbrella in it, or burying your face in a newspaper pretending to be engrossed in some story or the results of some stock, as if we are disturbing you when we walk by.

The truth of the matter is, if 600 dollars pays for a round trip ticket in coach, the price of a round trip first or business class ticket would be about 1,400 dollars. So, that "free" mixed drink that you are sipping on with the cute little umbrella just cost you 800 dollars! Enjoy it.

The other truth about flying in first class or business class is, if and when we crash, those of us flying in coach have a better chance of survival than you do in first class. Because, if you think about it, you never see the front of the airplane intact after an airplane crash, do you?

So, if we all do crash, please be sure to kiss the pilot on his butt cheek before you fly through his ass on your way through the front end of the airplane on an impact, and know that you will be providing a nice cushion for the rest of us who are ALL sitting behind you!

As U.S. Navy SEALs do a lot of traveling around the world for missions, special schools or training, the smart SEALs will join one of the many frequent flier programs so that he can get upgraded to business/first class. Because the government is not going to put an enlisted man who serves his country, even if he is returning from combat, in business or first class. Those seats are reserved for senior level officers, business executives, contractors, and the affluent. Get your butt to the back of the plane, soldier!

On one such training trip, a SEAL was ribbing another SEAL because he had accumulated enough frequent flier points to fly first class, and the other SEAL had to fly in coach. His brother SEAL was going on and on about all the free drinks he was going to have, and the hot meal he was going to eat while sitting in his nice soft seat with all that legroom.

Well, I guess that his conscience had gotten the better of him because while they were airborne, the SEAL in first class had the flight attendant send back a mixed drink to the SEAL that was flying in coach.

When the flight attendant went back to where the SEAL was sitting in coach, and offered the mixed drink to him, the SEAL in coach asked, "Who is this from?" The flight attendant replied that it was from the gentleman in first class. The SEAL replied, "That guy will just not leave me alone! I'm very sorry, miss, but could you please return that drink to him, and please tell him that I am straight, I like women not men, and tell him that I am not interested in having any sort of an affair with him."

The flight attendant replied, "I will certainly tell him, I am very sorry to disturb you, sir!"

The SEAL replied, "It is not your fault that he uses people like you to try to get what he wants."

When the stewardess returned the mixed drink and told the SEAL in first class what the SEAL in coach had said, the looks that the SEAL in first class got from the stewardess and the others flying in first class was priceless, especially when the gentleman sitting next to him in first class, got up and moved to another seat. Ahhh, paybacks can be so much fun.

Chapter 17

WHEN SEALS COCK BLOCK OTHER SEALS

When you are a single guy, and doing the bar scene, it is a tough enough game to play without someone undermining your efforts. Because not only do you have to contend with all the other competition inside the bar or nightclub, but also you never know who has your back, especially if you are in the SEAL teams and "out-on-the-town" in a SEAL platoon.

Our platoon was drinking in a local bar and having a great time together. Sitting at a table with some women were a few of the SEALs in our platoon, and they were making great time with the women who were seated with them. Myself and two other members of our platoon were sitting at the bar enjoying a few brews, as we admired the young studs making their moves on these women whom they were sitting with.

However, all of that was about to change when our platoon corpsman (Chuck) walked up to us and said, "Would you gents care to make a wager?"

"About what?" I asked.

Doc replied, "That I can make those women leave our SEAL teammates at that table over there."

Looking at Doc, and then at our SEAL brothers sitting at the table, I asked, "You're not going to make them puke are you?"

Doc laughed, "Nooo, nothing like that."

We all laughed as we recalled the episode with the Marines. Doc added, "No drugs, and nothing physical."

"OK, what is the bet?" I asked.

Doc replied, "If I win, you guys pay for my drinks, if I lose, I pay for yours."

I replied, "Nothing physical and no chemicals. OK, Doc, you're on. Go do your stuff." Doc smiled that "I got this bet" smile, and turned towards the poor souls sitting at the table.

Doc walked over to the table where the young SEALs were sitting and started chewing out the SEALs because they were sitting with the women, "Hey, I told you guys no drinking! You all got shots for syphilis, except you Greg, you got gonorrhea. You guys should not even be next to these women; you might infect them. Hey, they didn't kiss you did they? If they did I will have to give all you ladies shots as well!"

Greg stood and barked at Doc, saying, "What the hell are you talking about Doc? You know that is all bullshit!"

Doc fired back, saying, "Look, I am looking out for these women here. I am the medical corpsman and you guys are all infected from the hookers that you were with last week, so don't try to bullshit these women here that you are not infected! You women should take my advice, as I am their medical doctor, and leave these infected guys alone!" Doc spun around and left the table.

The women got that astonished look on their faces, and you could hear that they were shocked and clearly pissed off. The women got up from the table, yelling obscenities at the SEALs.

However, the funniest part was watching the SEALs trying to profess their innocence and purity to these women. SEALs… Pure? That is enough to make anyone laugh!

Doc knew that there is no rational woman on earth that would be willing to risk the chance of catching something from these guys! Doc also knew that being our platoon corpsman made him practically immune from any paybacks.

Had the whole scene not been so funny, I would have been pissed off too, because the night was young, and Doc drinks top-shelf Scotch.

Chapter 18

PAYBACK FOR BEING AN ASSHOLE PLATOON CHIEF

From time to time, every SEAL platoon will get a chief assigned to their platoon that is, quite frankly, just an asshole. Not that a platoon chief should always be a nice guy, but he should know that there is a time and a place to be an asshole to his men, and only when his men have asked for it (like any parent who has children). I received great advice from an officer who once told me, "Always praise your men in the open, and always chew their asses in private."

I remember one particular SEAL platoon chief named "Walter," and he did not quite master the fine art of knowing when and where to discipline his men, and he would rule them with an iron fist. The consequences for this type of "leadership" was not sitting well with the men in his platoon members, and "they" were forming plans to make Walter's life a bit interesting. So, his men, when faced with their platoon chief's open verbal abuses and usurpations, and feeling that they have been reduced to a form of despotism, his men decided to give their platoon chief paybacks.

The first payback to this chief came when one of his SEAL platoon members took a crap inside a plastic resealable bag; he then stabbed it numerous times with a pin, and then he sewed the "turd bag" inside his platoon chief's" pillow. Three of his SEAL platoon members then waited until lunch time, and with one acting as a lookout, the others snuck inside the chief's quarters onboard the ship, which was taking the SEAL platoon to their next area of operation that was about 30 days sailing time away. Once they found the rack (bed) that their chief was using to sleep on at night, they switched their chief's good pillow for the turd pillow.

Every night, Walter would go to sleep with his head on that smelly pillow. After a few days, the other chiefs that shared the chief's sleeping compartment started moving away from the area where Walter's rack was, and they commented to Walter about the foul odor emanating from his rack. Thinking that he had an old and somehow rotting mattress, Walter swapped out his old mattress for a new one. Walter thought that this would cure his smelly problem. However, for some illogical reason, he kept his "special" pillow.

One night, while Walter was sleeping in his bed, the plastic bag inside his pillow burst open and oozed out its smelly contents inside his pillow. The overpowering stench from the foul ooze woke Walter up, and he began to gag, and curse. Realizing that this had to be the actions of his own men, he punished every enlisted man in his SEAL platoon by putting all of them to work washing dishes in the ship's galley (better known as KP duty, "KP" meaning Kitchen Patrol).

When Walter's SEAL platoon arrived at their debarkation destination, I was there with my SEAL platoon to do a turnover of duties, after which my SEAL platoon was to be transported to another operational area. Both of our SEAL platoons were to spend about two weeks together, so there would be plenty of time to complete the turnover of duties and to have a few good times together as well.

One night, as I was returning from my night out in a local town, I was walking past the sauna room in our barracks. What caught my attention was a faint voice calling for help followed by a "thud" sound, "help… thud… help… thud… help…" When I walked into the room where the sauna was located, I saw that someone had tied the handles of the sauna door, which effectively prevented anyone on the inside of the sauna from getting out, and the temperature gauge to the sauna had been jammed on high. When I cut the rope away from the door handle and opened the door, there lying on the floor was Walter. Walter was very weak, and I had to take him to the base clinic for an IV, as he was dangerously dehydrated from being locked inside the sauna for so long.

As we were sitting there in the recovery room, I asked Walter how things were between him and his platoon. "Why, you think I got problems?" Smiling, I replied, "No, not at all Walter, I think that you being an asshole to your men all the time is working out great for you, don't you?"

Walter stared at the ceiling for some time while slowly nodding his head. He then said, "So, this is payback for me being an asshole to all of my men?" Yup, I replied, "It's up to you, Walter, you can sit down and work things out with your men, or you can continue being an asshole to them. Just remember this, Walter, the next time you might not be so lucky, because Lord knows, and from what I have heard from your men, they are willing to go to any length with their great imaginations to pay you back for being an asshole!"

I was glad to hear that Walter had eased up on being such a hard ass to his men in his platoon, and as a platoon, they were all doing a lot better.

Chapter 19

SOME MARRIAGES WERE JUST NOT MEANT TO BE

In the military, any marriage can be difficult because of the separation issues. Even so, marriages to guys in the U.S. Navy SEAL teams are extremely difficult. Most of the SEALs (the good ones anyway) do a lot of training and deploying, and it is a well-known fact that marriages in the U.S. Navy SEAL teams have the highest divorce rate in the Navy. You can ask any SEAL about marriages that they were a part of, which have gone bad, and usually there is a funny story behind it. (Well, it is funny after some time has passed.)

Like the story about Paul, when his ex-wife took a sledge-hammer to his motorcycle, then set his motorcycle on fire, and then threw all of his clothes out on the front lawn. Or, the officer who came home to his house after finishing a long deployment, only to find his house filled with new furniture, and a new couple living in what was once his house. As most SEALs give their wives a "Power of Attorney" (in the event a SEAL is killed or deployed for many months), this officer's ex-wife had sold the house and his dog while he was away on his deployment. He later learned that she left him for another man who would be at home more than an officer in the SEAL teams.

Such was the case with Mike, and his soon to be ex-wife. Mike's wife kept demanding that he stay home and stop deploying, or she would make his life in the SEAL teams extremely miserable for him, and she did. His wife would call the SEAL team compound every day while Mike was deployed, and ask to speak to the Commanding Officer. She would say that it is an emergency, and she would tell the SEAL commanding officer she was having anxiety attacks, and chest pains, and if the CO did not bring Mike home, she was going to die!

As you can imagine, this did create a few high profile problems for Mike. So, when Mike returned home early from his deployment at the request of the Commanding Officer, the CO told Mike to straighten out his home life or choose another career. Mike, not wanting to leave the SEAL teams, tried to reason with his wife, explaining that his SEAL career would be filled with deployments to other countries, and combat zones.

If she could not accept his career in the SEAL teams, then perhaps the best thing for the both of them is to divorce each other. To Mike's (and to the rest of us) amazement, she refused to accept his life in the SEAL teams, and any thought of a divorce. She told Mike that she was going to get her way, and not that f--king SEAL team.

Well, this started the infamous poop war. Every day, Mike would take a crap in their pet's cat box, and leave it for his wife to clean out, or he would take a crap from his upstairs condominium porch onto the porch of the people living below him before he went off to work every morning. When Mike was questioned about the poop on the porch, Mike would blame it on his wife.

I had asked Mike, "Don't you think your neighbors will know that it is you and not your wife who is taking a crap on their porch?" Mike replied, "Hey, she makes my life at the teams a living hell, so I am making her life at home a living hell. Besides, what are they going to do? Take the turd-a-ballistics to see if it came from my ass?"

This war went on for about a month, and the final straw came when Mike fell asleep after returning home from a night out with his teammates. The next day, when Mike did not show up for work at the SEAL team area, two SEALs from Mike's platoon were sent to Mike's house to check on him. When the two SEALs got there, they banged on Mike's door, and they heard Mike screaming from inside his house. The two SEALs kicked in Mike's front door, and they ran down the hall to where they heard Mike screaming.

When they got to Mike's bedroom, there was Mike tied spread-eagle to the four corners of his bed, and Mike was raving mad. He said that he had fallen asleep after some heavy drinking, and after he had an argument with his wife. When Mike woke up to go pee, he found that he could not move his entire body. Not only were Mike's arms and legs tied to the four corners of his bed, but his wife had also wrapped his body in plastic, and poured six bags of ready-mix concrete over his stomach, crotch area, and his legs.

Mike's SEAL platoon members had to use a sledge-hammer to free Mike from the hardened concrete. When Mike was finally cut free from his bonds, he took a much needed shower, as he did more than just piss on himself. When Mike came out of the shower, he called his wife at work to say that he had packed up all of his stuff, and that he was never coming back home. (After what she had done, what sensible man would?)

In the end, she lost! (However, in reality, she won, because in court, she got everything, the car, the house well, every-thing except Mike).

Chapter 20

WHAT DO YOU DO WITH A DRUNKEN SEAL/FROGMAN?

Now, who among us has not done something stupid whenever alcohol was involved? Well, besides having your fingernails painted with nail polish, or having a couple of eyes tattooed on the head of your penis, or had your penis pierced and then attached a tiny dinner bell to it (you know who you are). Because, when you get drunk, who wouldn't do those things?

When our platoon was deploying to a certain country in the Western Pacific, and we had a stopover in Hawaii, a few of us thought that it would be a great idea to "go-out-on-the-town and have a fun time trying to visit as many bars as we could before the light of day warmed our smiley faces." After all, who knows what perils awaited us at our final destination.

I must say that although Hawaii is a nice place, it is also extremely expensive to have a great time as a sailor out on the town. We found the cheapest bars that we could, where the beer cost us $1.00 a bottle (in the 1970s, the same beer in a similar bar in San Diego would have been around 35 cents). Prices be damned, we were all having a great time, and Lord knows where the time goes when you are having so much fun. To this day, I am not sure what possessed us to go swimming in a small fountain in front of this huge house. However, at the time I guess that it seemed like a good idea.

There we all were, sitting in this fountain, singing songs, and sharing a bottle of Scotch, when we were so rudely interrupted by two huge figures. The largest figure spoke up first and said, "We got a tank, but it isn't full of water!" We all looked up at him through the water spraying down on us from the fountain, and you could make out a badge, a gun, and a car with pretty flashing lights on it. "Hooya, police officers!" we replied.

Tim spoke up and said, "We don't mean no harm officers, tomorrow we are shipping out of here, and this was just a little celebration is all." The officers looked down at us and said, "That's fine boys, but this fountain is part of our Governor's mansion. How about we take you gentlemen back to your base, or would you like us to take you to our tank to finish your swim?" We all replied, "Oh, the base would be great officers, thank you very much, yes the base, we must go back to the base!"

As the police officers were driving us back to the military base, a car pulled up alongside of us at a traffic light, and the people inside that car started to look at us in the back of the police patrol car. Tim yelled at the people, "Hey, what the f--k are you looking at? I got your license plate number you assholes, and when I get out, I am going to come to your house!"

The people in the car made a left turn and sped away from us. Tim was laughing; he apologized to the officers, saying, "Sorry, officers, I just couldn't resist." The officers were laughing too and said, "No problem, we decided that we are going to take all of you to jail so you can sleep it off. Thanks a lot, Tim!

Chapter 21

KICKED OUT OF FRANCE

Now, one might find it difficult to be working in a foreign country where some of the people are arrogant, speak a different language, and do not care for Americans. However, you should realize, like in most countries, there are always some bad people mixed in with the good, and not everyone hates Americans. However, in human nature, the ones that do hate Americans leave a bad impression on you about the rest of them.

Our platoon was sent to a base in France, where we were all going to conduct joint training with the French Navy Commandos. The French Navy Commandos are the Special Forces of the French Navy. When we were stationed on their military base, many of us had to adjust to their military protocol. The French Navy Commandos were all about military rank. For example, inside their dining hall facility, everyone eats and sits according to military rank, i.e., all enlisted eat according to their military rank. The first to eat among the enlisted ranks are the E-8 and 7s, then the E-6s, then the E-5s and E-4s and so on down the military rank scale. There is no difference in the amount or the quality of the food which everyone eats. Nevertheless, I did not like the idea that the lowest ranks ate their food last, as it is our belief in the SEAL teams that you take care of your men, and you lead by example.

As I was the chief of our platoon with the Enlisted rank of E-7 (E-7 is on a scale from E-1 up to E- 9, with E-9 being the highest of the enlisted rank), I entered the French dining hall in my dress white uniform as per their military protocol. On this particular French military naval base, eating was a formal affair. I sat at the designated seating area for E-7s, and the meal started pleasantly enough with French bread and bottles of red wine being placed on our dining tables.

As I did not speak French, I asked the Chief Sergeant, who was sitting across from me, to "pass me the butter."

The Chief Sergeant responded to me in English by saying, "You stupid American, it is called beurre! Say it! Beurre! You are in my country, you stupid American, so speak my language! Say beurre!"

Of course, his attitude really pissed me off. As I began to feel the rage of my anger swelling up inside me from his insulting demeanor, and being the wonderful diplomat that I am, I looked at this asshole and said, "OK, burr, like a burr in my ass!" I came across the table; I knocked him out of his chair and threw him on the ground. I began punching his face and yelling, "Here's a burr for ya, Frenchy!"

I guess a logical man would have surveyed his surroundings and seen that he was greatly outnumbered, and a logical man would have ignored his insults and walked out. However, at this point in my anger, I was way beyond being logical. Before I knew it, the French Navy Commandos, who were all inside the dining hall, came to the rescue of their comrade and began kicking and punching me from all sides. I felt pain in my ribs, and the occasional slight blackout from being kicked or punched in the back of my head. I knew that I was going to be in a lot of trouble if I did not make my way to an exit door and escape.

I was trying to fight my way out to the exit door as best as I could, but I was getting beat really bad. When I finally made it to the exit door, I was on my hands and knees; I pushed the dining hall door open, and I crawled outside. I heard one of my guys yell, "Chief! Those bastards are beating our chief, come on, let's get em!" It took all I had to yell at my guys to stop, and when it was all over, I was in handcuffs being led away to their brig (jail).

When my officers came to see me in the brig on the French Navy base, they wanted to know how it all had happened, and I told them the truth. They said that they were going to see the base Contre-Amiral (an officer in charge of the entire French Navy base with a U.S. military rank equivalent to a commodore or rear admiral), and try to straighten this whole matter out. My officers sent our platoon corpsmen into my cell to check me out and treat my wounds. The corpsman said that I probably had a couple of busted ribs, and he gave me some pills for pain. In a low voice so that our officers could not hear, he asked me about payback for what happened to me. I looked at him and said, "I like the thought, but do not do anything yet."

When my officers returned that night to give me an update on my dilemma, they informed me that at 0800 hours in the morning, I was to go before the base rear admiral for a formal hearing on my serious misconduct in the dining hall. I was also informed that due to the serious nature of this "international incident," there was going to be a representative from the U.S. embassy military group that would also be in attendance.

The morning came as it always does, and at 0800 sharp there I was standing at attention in the rear admiral's office wearing my torn, bloodstained, dress white uniform with both of my officers, and the gentleman from the U.S. embassy military group, who was one of our senior U.S. military representatives in France.

The rear admiral was slowly shaking his head while looking over the report about the incident that took place in the dining hall. When he had completed reading the report he took in a deep breath and exhaled with a slow frustrated sound. The French rear admiral looked at me, and asked me to explain my actions. As I began my explanation, the rear admiral leaned back in his office chair and stared up at his ceiling fan while listening to my entire explanation about my actions in the dining hall. While I was explaining my side of the story about what had happened, he began to frown and shake his head. The more details that I brought to light about the incident in the dining hall, the more aggravated the rear admiral became about what I was saying.

When I had finished explaining about how the entire event had unfolded, the rear admiral leaned forward in his chair, looked at me in total disgust, and said, "If you are to remain here on my base, you will write a formal letter of apology to me about this incident. You will also apologize to my entire commando unit for your insubordinate, disgraceful, and disrespectful actions as a representative of your U.S. military. Should you choose not to carry out what I am demanding from you, I will request that this gentleman, from your U.S. embassy, escort you off of my base, and out of my country."

While I was standing there at attention, and looking at this rear admiral, I started to feel that what this rear admiral was requesting me to do was a lot of bullshit. I truly felt that I was not the guilty one here, as I was not the one who set the entire event in motion inside the dining hall. Well, as I am a warrior and not a diplomat, I looked at both of my officers who were standing next to me, and they both appeared to have that "It's up to you, Chief" look on their faces. Saying nothing, I smiled at them both.

I then looked at the rear admiral and said, "Sir, nothing would please me more than to go to another country, where the BULLSHIT doesn't stink like it does right here in your office!"

Upon hearing this, the rear admiral shot out of his chair, yelling, "OUT! GET HIM OUT OF MY SIGHT! GET HIM OUT OF MY COUNTRY!" The rear admiral yelled a few other words at me in French that I am sure were not complimentary, but in French, somehow it sounded that way.

As I was being escorted away by the gentleman from the U.S. embassy, my officers looked at me and said, "Jesus, Chief, we didn't expect you to say that!"

I looked at both of my officers and said, "Sirs, take care of the men, and tell them that I do NOT want any of them to do any paybacks for this!"

For my sins, I was sent to Spain for three weeks, where I waited for my platoon to join me after they had completed their joint training exercises with the French commandos.

Ahhh, Sangria, paella, and the sweet sounds of Spanish guitars...

Chapter 22

WHEN HYPNOTISM GOES BAD

Sometimes, the guys in the SEAL teams come up with some truly great ideas for a joke that the normal person would never dare carry out. Probably because most SEALs have seen and done such terrible things in the performance of their duties that most would do anything for a good laugh to help them forget all the tragedies of war.

Our platoon was on a training mission at a remote area out in the Imperial Valley of California, where several groups of Marines were trying to locate and destroy or capture our platoon before we reached our intended target. Our mission was a success, as we had just completed the 16-day reconnaissance patrol evading all the Marines, and we were all ready to just relax over a few beers at our base camp. As we were sitting there telling funny stories about a few of our SEAL brothers, one of our platoon members started telling us about a bar in El Centro, California, that he had been to before. According to Ben's story, it would seem that this particular bar had a hypnotist for their main act. It seems that this particular hypnotist could hypnotize men into thinking that they were pregnant. We all thought that it would be funny to take his act to the next level, without the knowledge of the hypnotist.

So, we loaded up the moulage kit. This is a medical training kit made up of fake wounds that you would attach to your body. These fake wounds had the ability to pump out blood from wherever the wound was attached by the person wearing the wound. After loading up all the fake wounds that we would need for our practical joke, we jumped into our pickup truck, and we all headed to the bar in El Centro that had the hypnotist as their main attraction.

Little did this poor hypnotist know that this was going to be one hell of a night for everyone who was going to be there to see his act, to include our act as well. We were all laughing in the parking lot outside of the club as Ben and Paul opened the Moulage Kit and took out what each of them wanted for wounds, and put them into their pockets. Ben and Paul walked inside the club ahead of us and headed to the restroom to fill up their blood mix bags, and to put on their simulated wounds, which they concealed under their shirts.

It was also agreed that Doug and Steve would conceal their KA-BAR knives (these knives had a six-inch blade), and when Dr. Moore asked for volunteers, Doug and Steve would go up on stage to be hypnotized by the "Great Dr. Moore." There all we were, sitting at the front row table, drinking and going over our plan, laughing at what was about to unfold.

The announcer came out on the stage and introduced the Great Dr. Moore. After Dr. Moore went into some BS details about how only a person with a sophisticated mind can be hypnotized, Ben and Paul went to the bathroom to glue on their wounds for our performance.

When the Great Dr. Moore asked for a few volunteers to come up on his stage to be hypnotized, of course Doug and Steve jumped up, and went onto the stage. The prearranged signal that we had for Doug and Steve to show us that they were indeed NOT hypnotized was to keep lifting their right finger every ten seconds.

Once Dr. Moore had everyone hypnotized (or so he thought), the audience was having a great time laughing at whatever Dr. Moore requested his hypnotized subjects to do. Even so, things were about to go very wrong for this poor doctor, because when the Great Dr. Moore said, "Now, all the men are pregnant and are about to give birth," Steve and Doug pulled out their KA-BAR knives and started screaming that they were going to kill the guys who got them pregnant!

Doug and Steve yelled obscenities to the back of the room where Paul and Ben were standing by the restroom. Doug and Steve pulled out their knives and jumped off the stage and charged towards Paul and Ben in the back of the room and started attacking both of them with their knives.

Some of the people thought that it was all part of the act, until there was a lot of screaming by Ben and Paul. The spectators who saw the blood squirting out from Ben's wounds made everyone's screaming worse. When several people saw Paul's fake knife wound squirting out blood, one woman screamed, "They're really killing them!"

The Great Dr. Moore was in shock, standing on stage with his mouth open as he watched the entire bloody scene unfold in front of him. Dr. Moore kept yelling, "When I clap my hands, you will awaken!" CLAP CLAP. "When I clap my hands, you will awaken!" CLAP CLAP.

Steve and Doug chased Paul and Ben out of the club, as people were screaming and running everywhere, especially away from Steve and Doug with their knives, and they were still screaming that they were going to kill the guys who got them pregnant. We all ran out of the club and got into our truck. We waited in the parking lot for a few moments as we heard and saw everyone in the place screaming, and running out of the exit doors.

None of us knew what had happened until later, as we had all sped away in our truck, and returned to our remote desert camp. We enjoyed laughing and recounting the evening's events about our little joke while we drove down the road to our base camp. We were glad that no one got hurt in the stampede of people making for the exits, and we were all certain that the Great Dr. Moore's career got a boost from our acting.

Well, it is either that, or he will not be telling men that they are pregnant anymore.

Chapter 23

DRUNK AGAIN, CHIEF? WELL, NOW IT'S PAYBACK TIME

Training out in our desert base camp was always great. Why? Because for any of our SEAL training, we had a 360 degree free-fire zone for shooting live ammunition, we never had to pick up any brass (the expended bullet casings), and we had no limit on the amount of explosives we could use or where we wanted to place them. It was also great because everyone trained hard and everyone played hard.

Going through the final phase of your SEAL pre-deployment training is long, about four to six weeks (depending on the type and location of training). As instructors, we all had a great time out there training platoons in the desert, and every Saturday night we all went into the small desert town and enjoyed the local culture at the bar.

Whenever you drink, most of the guys know when enough is enough. Carl was a good SEAL, and he was also a good training chief, but he had a small problem finding the toilet whenever he got really drunk. One time, when Carl came back from the town, thinking that he was in the restroom, he peed on my wall locker and on my bed, waking me up to a golden shower. I yelled at Carl, "You asshole, what the f--k is wrong with you?"

Carl slurred, "Oh crap, Billy! Sorry, man, I thought I was in the toilet!"

One night, I decided to stay back at camp, because I felt that it was time for a little payback on Carl for having peed on me, my wall locker, and my bed. After all, fair is fair. So I got a small roll of thin wire and a 50 cap blasting machine (a 50 cap blasting machine is capable of producing up to 100 volts of electricity, enough power to fire 50 blasting caps at once). I stripped down Carl's bed, ran the wires to the center of his mattress, and stripped the ends of the wires bare. Once the wires were in place on the center of his mattress, I poured water on his mattress and put his sheets back on the bed. I hid the rest of the wire under his bed and rigged a quick disconnect (so that I could pull on the wires, and they would come loose, and Carl would not be able to trace the location of the operator... me). I then ran the wire leads behind several lockers and beds to my location, and taped the wires to my bed for easy access. When I was finished, I joined the rest of the guys in town.

After a good time in town, we all returned to our base camp. I climbed into my rack (bed) and pretended to drift off to sleep. It was about two hours later when Carl came stumbling in. He took off his clothes and fell into his bed. As Carl laid on his stomach in his bed, I quietly removed the electric blasting machine from under my pillow. I slowly connected the wires taped to my bed to the electric blasting machine and pushed down on the green button. When I pushed down on the green button, I could hear the internal capacitors charging up.

When the amber light came on, this alerted me there was enough electricity to fire 50 blasting caps (or 100 volts of electricity). I pushed the red button down to release the 100-volt electric charge…

"UGH," came the verbal sound of success!

I watched as Carl rolled over and sat half up in his bed, and he was feeling his stomach area. He lay back down on his bed, only this time he was on his back. I waited for a few moments for Carl to get comfortable, and again, I pushed down on the green button. I could hear the capacitors charging up. The amber light came on alerting me there was enough electricity to fire, so I pushed the red button again…

Carl screamed out, "AHHH, What the f--k is shocking me!" I could hardly contain my urge to laugh aloud.

Carl got out of his bed and pulled his mattress off the frame of his bed. While Carl was doing that, I pulled on the quick disconnect and reeled in all the wires as quickly as I could. He found two thin wires in his mattress and started cursing at everyone around his bed. I pretended to wake up and asked, "What the hell is going on?" Carl was blabbering something about wires, and getting shocked by someone. I turned on the lights and said, "Do you see any wires going to someone's bed, Carl?" Of course, there were none to be found. I told him to go back to bed, and we would all talk about it in the morning.

When everyone drifted off to sleep, I took my blasting machine and wires back out to the bunker area, as there was surely going to be a search in the morning. When morning came, there was no evidence, and no proof. Carl was only left with suspicions. (Well, until now. Sorry, Carl, but now we are even!)

Chapter 24

WHEN A SEAL BROTHER STEALS MILK OR ICE CREAM

Whenever SEALs deploy to a remote area to conduct training, where certain items will be hard to get, a few of us would stock up on those items so that we could enjoy them after a day of hard training out in the field or after coming in from the heat of the desert sun.

Drinking someone else's milk or eating their ice cream might sound a bit inconsequential to some of you out there. However, I can tell you that among certain members in the SEAL teams, it really IS a big deal. You have to understand that when you are going through advanced training in a SEAL platoon or as instructors out in the hot desert for a month or more on a limited budget, you may have little funds for luxury items like milk or ice cream, and you cannot run into town every night, because you will most likely be out in the field training at all hours.

Sometimes, during your training, it can get up to 120 degrees under the hot summer sun, and for lunch or dinner, you eat MREs (you remember those... MRE = Meal Ready to Eat — you just add hot water to the freeze-dried food in the plastic bag, shake it up — yum!). However, instead of eating a hot MRE, you might want to come in from the heat of the day and sit down to a little ice cream, or chug a few huge gulps of your cold milk before eating. Because these items are rare in a training environment out in the middle of the hot desert, let alone in combat.

With that in mind, when SEALs deploy to a remote training area as instructors, they would all put their foodstuffs into common refrigerators that are inside the instructors' lounge. This creates an environment where there will be one or two guys who will steal food and drinks from the other guys. This is all because they did not bring enough money to support themselves. In the old days of the SEAL teams (late 60s and early 70s), if a SEAL put a lock on his locker, a brother SEAL would ask him, "Why are you putting a lock on your locker? Are you calling me a thief?" It is sad to see that times and events have changed people.

Eric was that typical petty thief, and everyone knew it was him when it came to helping himself to our foodstuffs. Eric was a good SEAL, but he was a weasel when it came to our milk and ice cream.

I give total credit to my SEAL brother Frank for coming up with the best deterrent for a food and drink thief. One day, during our lunch break, Frank came into the instructors' lounge where we were all sitting around and talking about the day's training events. Frank went to the common refrigerator, and took out his one-gallon jug of milk and his container of ice cream. Frank then placed the milk and ice cream on the table in front of everyone.

What happened next was pure genius. Frank unzipped his pants and took out his penis. Frank proceeded to rub his penis all around the opening of his milk jug; he then stuck his penis inside his ice cream container and into his ice cream. Frank then put his milk container and his ice cream back into the refrigerator.

Frank looked over at Eric and said, "If you want to taste my dick, Eric, help yourself!" We all laughed out loud. Then, as we were all sitting there, it hit us. We all got up and went to the refrigerators to do exactly what Frank had done in front of Eric.

It must have worked, because none of us were missing anything after that.

Chapter 25

FOGGY ICE CUBES

During one of our many Joint Unconventional Warfare exercises that are held overseas, our platoon was tasked with conducting a few joint training exercises with several different Special Forces units who are our allies from various countries. All of the missions are extremely challenging, and after each mission, there was a good time to be had by all who were involved. After one of our joint missions, at one of our "letting off steam" beach parties, one group from a certain country thought that it would be funny (without us knowing about it) to piss in a few of the pitchers of beer that the Aussies (Australian - Special Air Service or SAS) and ourselves (the SEALs) were drinking.

The next day, this particular Special Forces unit all had a good laugh at us when they told us what they had done (Big Mistake). Now, I enjoy a good prank as much as the next person does. However, the thought of this particular prank still makes me gag. What was going to be the vengeance for pissing in our beer? Well, the Aussies and a few of my SEAL platoon members got together and made some foggy ice cubes (just wait). Four days had passed since the piss in the beer joke on both the Australian SAS and our SEAL platoon. On the evening of the fifth day the Aussies and my platoon members decided to throw a party on the beach with bottled beer, hard mixed drinks, and of course, the foggy ice cubes to go with all the mixed drinks.

When I arrived at the beach party, an Aussie friend came up to me and told me to drink only the bottled beer, and under NO circumstances whatsoever was I to ingest any of the ice cubes!

As the night went on, the guys who pissed in our beers were having a great time drinking the mixed drinks and chewing on the foggy ice cubes; all through the night, they kept mixing more drinks and adding more foggy ice cubes to their drinks. The Aussies and my platoon members would laugh whenever they saw one of the guys that pissed in our beer chewing on the ice cubes. It all seemed pleasant, and everyone was having a great time. So, I pressed my Aussie friend for information about why I could not drink anything with the ice cubes.

What he whispered to me was something that was so gross that maggots would gag if they had heard. He leaned close to me and whispered, "Well, mate, it would seem that a couple of days ago, a few of our boys got together and had a 'wanking' party in the ice cube trays, and unlike those blokes that pissed in our beers, we aren't admitting to nothing. So, sit back mate, and enjoy our little payback for the piss in the beer."

I could hardly contain myself about the whole matter. It was no wonder that the Aussies and my guys would laugh whenever they saw a guy chewing on the ice cubes, or take a sip from his mixed drink. There is no doubt that drinking piss in beer was much better than this.

Note to self: Never use ice cubes if you do not know who made them!

The following day was an exercise in low-level terrain flying inside a C-130 aircraft. This aircraft, in my opinion, is just about the best thing to fly in if you are going on a tactical mission, and the relationships that any special unit has with the C-130 crews are always professional ones. The C-130 crews are well known professionals that will do anything to get you in or out of a target area.

Flying inside the C-130 is a wild ride, as the C-130 would fly just a few feet off the ground or what the Air Force calls "nape of the earth terrain flying." All the hair would stand up on the back of your neck when you saw how close to the ground you were flying. The reason for flying this low is so that the aircraft can fly under the enemy's radar, and get you in or out of your target area undetected.

Each group of special operations personnel boarded the C-130 to be flown around in a racetrack pattern that went over the ocean, through a huge valley, and then back to the landing strip. These low level flights took a lot of time, and it was getting late. By the time that it was our platoon's turn to go on the next flight, the loadmaster on the C-130 came out and said that we were going to be the last ones to go on this flight because it was getting late. This meant that the Australian SAS team would not get the experience of the low-level flight.

As our platoon had done this many times in the past, we asked the Aussies if they would like to take our place on the last run. They were very grateful to us for offering, and they said that when they got back from the flight that the beers would be on them.

We watched as our Aussie friends took off in the C-130 and flew low level across the ocean towards the designated valley. The C-130 was almost out of our sight when we all witnessed a huge fireball. Our entire platoon was stunned at what we were seeing and we all knew that it meant only one thing: The C-130 had crashed. We all ran to our truck to go over to the boat unit and take a couple of our swift boats over to what we knew was going to be a crash site.

When everyone finally got the word out about the crash, we had several boats and helicopters covering the entire crash area. At the crash site, we found chunks of debris from the aircraft that were scattered and floating about, and it was indeed a miracle that we found an air crewman who was still alive. The sad part was that he was the only one that we had found; there was nothing but a few chunks of debris floating in the water and any other bodies, or body parts, were nowhere to be seen or found.

Our platoon felt bad that we had offered up our turn on the C-130 to our Aussie friends who were now all dead. Even so, we also knew that they would have done the same for us. It is always difficult to lose friends. However, we will never forget them, nor will we forget the jokes and good times that we had all shared together as brothers in arms, for when we close our eyes we can see their young faces, and if we listen hard, we can still hear their laughter as we watched those guys chewing on the foggy ice cubes.

Chapter 26

NAVY SEALS BLOW UP A UFO

One of the many times that I was a camp guard out at our remote training area in the California desert, I got to thinking about how to mess with the minds of the local lizard people that lived near our training area. Remember, kids, every good joke is achieved with a good plan and good preparation.

One day while Roger and I were just sitting around, bored, and having a few beers together, we came up with the idea to create a UFO out on the bombing range near the base of Lion Head Mountain, in an attempt to scare the people who were living in nearby "Slab City." Slab City got its name from all the concrete slabs left over from a WWII camp, "Camp Dunlop," that had supported the now long gone wooden structures of the deserted camp.

We had plenty of target material to blow up, which was left over from the last SEAL platoon's training cycle, and we also had a small portable field generator, which we used to power our targets for training. After identifying everything that we needed for our UFO, we then loaded up everything around our camp to build our UFO, including all the explosives to blow it up. Once our truck was completely loaded, we headed out onto the bombing range near Lion Head Mountain (about 4 miles from the location of our intended spectators).

The access road that led out to Lion Head Mountain is near Slab City, the place where all the lizard people or snowbirds live (people who park their motor homes and live near the bombing range to escape the snow up north). It was about 4:00 p.m. when we arrived at our chosen site at the base of Lion Head Mountain, and we got right to work constructing our UFO.

We strung up white and blue lights that would slowly pulse on and off, and we set timers to shoot starburst flares that would launch sideways. We also set up a system to drop white smoke grenades that, once they started smoking, we thought the lights would reflect off of the white smoke, creating an eerie glow. We also hooked up an old siren that we adjusted to make a low "wobbling" sound. When we were all finished constructing our UFO, it was just about dark.

We started our portable generator, and set the final timer for 30 minutes, which would activate all the lights, timers, and the siren. When we were satisfied that everything was set up and would function properly, we got into our truck and headed to Slab City, where most of the lizard people lived in their motor homes.

When we arrived at Slab City, we walked up to the top of a large sand berm, which was left there from the construction of the Coachella Canal. We looked at our watches, and we noticed that we had about five minutes left before the timers would activate everything on our UFO, so we started jumping up and down and yelling in excitement, "UFO! UFO!" People started to leave their motor homes, and they ran up to where we were standing and pointing.

"Where do you see it? Where's the UFO?"

Roger yelled out, "It just landed over there!" All the lizard people and snowbirds were scanning the desert area, trying to sight the UFO.

When the timers activated, and the lights came on, the low wobbling sound of the siren could be heard. You would have thought that Jesus Christ himself had just appeared. One of the lizard people yelled out, "Oh my God! There it is! There it is!"

"Listen, you can hear it! Hey everyone, it's an honest to God, UFO!"

More snowbirds and lizard people came running up to the top of the sand berm where we were all standing and pointing at the UFO, listening to the wobbling sound, and watching the lights pulse on and off through the haze of the white smoke from our smoke grenades.

"What do you think they are doing out there?"

My partner in crime said, "I don't know, but we are going to go out there and find out. This is a government bombing range, and we are the only ones who are allowed out there. Everyone remain calm, and stay here until we get back!"

As we walked down the berm towards our truck, someone yelled out, "You boys be careful now!"

We got into our truck and drove out to our UFO site. As we got near it, Roger started to turn his headlights on and off, and when we got close to our UFO, he left the lights off as if the UFO had caused some sort of power loss to our truck.

We got out of our truck just as the starburst flares went off. It was so funny, because we could only imagine what the lizard people were all thinking and saying. We planted our explosive charges and cut the time fuse for two minutes. We got back into our truck and drove off in a different route, across the desert towards our base camp with our lights off so that the lizard people could not see us leave the UFO area.

When the explosive charges went off, we started laughing. Roger said, "Many people will tell you stories about UFOs, but few will tell you they actually saw one land, and then be attacked by the government," or so we thought.

In town the next day, the news in the bars and the restaurants were buzzing about the UFO that had landed out in the desert, and how the Navy SEALs went out there and blew it up. We heard comments like, "This is just another damn government cover-up, just like that flying saucer that crashed out in Roswell!" and "I guess those Navy SEALs do not know a damn thing about diplomacy!" "Those SEALs always just shoot first, and ask questions later!"

OK, you snowbirds and lizard people, if you are reading this, I know you won't believe it, but it really was a joke!

Chapter 27

COMBAT IS EASIER THAN POLITICS

Being in the SEAL teams, or for that matter, any special unit, will bring you in contact with all kinds of people, though mostly it will be with the bad guys. However, there will be a few occasions in a Navy SEAL's career when it is not just the enemy that will look at a Navy SEAL or a "special warfare operator" as a bad guy. Sometimes, it will be the very people that you (as a member of the U.S. military) have been sworn to protect and defend that will look at you as if you are the bad guy, or an expensive item that needs to be cut out of the Department of Defense's budget.

A few years back, when I was in Central America, and during the course of my many intelligence briefings and debriefings, I became friends with our U.S. Ambassador. One day, he invited me to one of his formal "ambassador balls." To my credit (and defense), I tried to refuse the ambassador's invitation, not once, but several times. I told him that I did not think I would be comfortable in a political setting, as the ambassador's guests were to include the host country's president, members of his staff, and members of his family, high-ranking officers and their families, and other high officials of that government.

The U.S. Ambassador said, "Nonsense, these people would love to meet someone like you, and to talk with you about what you have accomplished here for them."

Again, I stressed, "Sir, you should really reconsider, as I am very rough around the edges."

The ambassador simply responded, "You will be there in your dress uniform with all of your medals, and that is that."

I replied, "Yes, Mr. Ambassador."

On the night of the ambassador's ball, I boarded a military helicopter, and I was off to the capital to attend the ambassador's ball. Arriving at night in my dress white uniform, I felt like such a target. I thought to myself, If I came under an enemy attack, I would have to jump into a mud puddle and roll around in it to darken my uniform so that I would be able to hide from the enemy. I arrived at the designated location for the ambassador's ball; I had gotten there early, and luckily so did the bartender.

I do not know why people go to these types of functions, unless they are ALL obligated to go. I thought they must be. When the ambassador arrived he walked up to me, and we briefly greeted each other. Again I stressed my concern about being here, and again, he said, "Relax, just be yourself, and enjoy the night!"

OK, a word of advice to all you political types out there, those words should never be spoken to any U.S. Navy SEAL at a formal function, unless he is ONLY there with other SEALs or Spec Ops (Special Operations) types. As I was leaning on the end of the bar, and looking around, I realized that the evening was nice but it was terribly formal. Everyone was nodding at each other, adhering to proper political protocols (of which I knew very little), letting out the occasional phony laughs, and pretending to be interested in whatever conversations that were going on with each select group of people.

As I was finishing my drink, and planning my clandestine escape out of this place (but not soon enough), I watched as a young woman approached me. She was quite lovely, all dressed up in her beautiful gown and jewels. Smiling at me, she said, "I am Miss Constanza." She then asked who I might be. I told her that I was one of the U.S. trainers in her country, and that I was working with the Navy commandos in the southern part of her country. I was shocked by her response.

With a slight frown on her face she said, "Really? I find the enlisted men in our military to be poor and uneducated fools, don't you?"

Well, a smarter man (who would know when to keep his big mouth shut) would have excused himself to the restroom. But hey, I never walked around saying that I am a smart man, and those of you who know me, know that given this woman's statement, I could not just walk away or stand there and say nothing about her remark.

I looked at this young woman of wealth and stature, all dressed up in her jewels and flowing gown, and I said, "Poor and uneducated fools? Lady, I would much rather be with those poor and uneducated enlisted members of your military than to be standing here next to a woman like you, who thinks so little about the people fighting for your country and your freedom. They may be poor and uneducated fools to you, but to me, they are the salt of the earth, and you, señorita, you're nothing more than a spoiled little snob, so do me a big favor and piss off."

A look of utter contempt for me came over her face, and she threw the contents of her glass (red wine) on my dress white uniform (staining my white uniform and my white shoes). I watched her as she spun around, and walked directly over to the president of her country.

"Oh shit," I whispered to myself, as I watched her speaking with the president and pointing at me. The president looked at me (with one of those "You're so screwed looks"), and then the president motioned with his finger at the U.S. ambassador (like a parent to a kid who did something wrong).

I watched the U.S. Ambassador walk over to the president with a look of concern on his face. I was beginning to feel ill as this large group of high-ranking officials, and the president of the country were all looking at me, and listening to the young woman whom I had just insulted, and who was now crying and pointing at me. It was then for the first time in my professional life among so many political people that I saw it happen: The proverbial shit hit the fan. Remember how you felt when you knew you were in trouble? Well, this feeling was much worse.

This entire group of high-ranking officials all walked over to me, and as I stood there in my wine-stained dress white uniform, the U.S. ambassador spoke first. "Chief, please tell me that this was just a simple misunderstanding, and please tell me that you did not insult the president's niece."

I thought to myself — The president's niece? I am so screwed!

As I began to speak, the president interrupted me, saying, "Stop." He then looked at me as if I was next to be executed, and in a very cold voice he said, "Chief, please repeat to me exactly, word for word, what you said to my niece."

As I was repeating the entire encounter that I had with the president's niece, I subconsciously realized that I could turn up missing, or I could have some plausible fatal accident ordered by anyone in this group of officials.

When I was finished explaining what I had said (and not why I said it) to the president's niece, I looked at the president and said, "Mr. President, had I known that this beautiful young lady was your niece, I would have chosen my words much more carefully. I apologize to your niece, to you, Mr. President, and to all of you here for my harsh and disrespectful words to Miss Constanza."

The U.S. ambassador looked at me with a look of disappointment (which, as his friend, hurt. Because I was the one that was the source of his embarrassment), and then he turned to the president and said, "Mr. President, allow me to escort the chief out of here, as his presence is no longer welcome."

As the ambassador and I walked towards the exit, I said to the ambassador, "I tried to warn you, sir, but you insisted that I come here."

The ambassador looked at me and said, "You're no diplomat, Billy, but I admire your heart. Have a safe trip back to your base."

Safe trip back, I thought. Yeah, right. I did not sleep that night as I moved from hotel to hotel with all my weapons, waiting to be attacked by anyone. When I got back to my base, I slept armed, and inside my barricaded room.

The next day I received a radio call from the office of military intelligence. I was ordered to go up to the military command post and to wait there. I was further informed that there was a major from intelligence coming in on a helicopter, and this major wanted to speak with me about a personal matter. A feeling of doom washed over me as I got into my jeep and drove up to the helicopter landing pad next to the military command post where I was to wait for my "visitor."

I parked my jeep at the end of the helicopter landing pad, and I waited there with my submachine gun and my 9mm pistol. If I was to die, I was going to go down fighting. It was not long before I heard the unmistakable sound of the UH-1 helicopter flying in. The helicopter circled around the command post once, and I watched as the helicopter slowly landed, facing me. Four military guards from the command post ran up to the helicopter to provide security for its occupants.

A female from intelligence, wearing the rank of a major, stepped out of the helicopter, and all the military guards snapped to attention. I watched as this female major slowly looked around the helicopter landing pad area, as if she was evaluating the security around her.

When she spotted me standing next to my jeep, she started walking towards me with her armed guards. When she got near, I saluted her, and I identified myself. She did not return my salute as per proper military protocol. She took off her flight helmet, looked at me, smiling, and said, "I am Major Constanza, and I am the mother of the young woman you insulted at your ambassador's ball the other night."

As I was looking at her, I thought to myself, shit, this is it, they are going to toss me out of a helicopter flying at 5,000 feet.

"My daughter has told me about the comment she made to you, and what you said to her at your ambassador's ball. I flew down here to personally thank you for your passionate words, about how you feel about our men with whom you are training in our military. My daughter has a lot to learn, and I am sorry for her actions the other night."

Looking at the major, I said, "Ma'am, there is no apology necessary."

Smiling, she added, "I am also ordered to pass on to you from my brother, the president; he wants you to stay away from my daughter. I do not think that this will be a problem. Do you?"

Taking in a slow deep breath, I said, "No, Ma'am. None whatsoever."

Again, she smiled at me, and after putting her flight helmet back on, she saluted me and said, "Goodbye, Chief, and take care of yourself."

As she started to become airborne in her helicopter, I saluted her again, and I was thinking to myself: Combat is so much easier than politics.

Chapter 28

HEMORRHOID PATROL

Hard training in the SEAL teams is always the key to the success of any real mission, though at times some training missions teetered on the ridiculous side.

On this particular training mission, we were to simulate blowing up a bridge with simulated explosive charges. This bridge, which went across the Mississippi River connecting Highway 84, was a key route for supplying the enemy. We had seven days to recon the bridge, and after we had assessed how much explosives that we would need to blow it up, we were to call in our requirements by radio, and a friendly agent would meet us with the required amount of simulated explosives (made from clay), and anything else that we would need to complete our mission.

On or about our third night patrolling through the swamps that surrounded the bridge area, something started to hang out of my butt, and it was not poo poo. As I am not a doctor, and as I had never had a hemorrhoid before, this was a new experience for me. Not knowing what it was, I dropped my pants and tried to pinch it off, thinking it might be a big leech or a tick. However, when I squeezed it as hard as I could, nothing came out. So, I tried to pull on it but that just increased the pain. Frustrated about what was causing me so much pain, I went to our platoon corpsman (Doc); still thinking it might be a leech or a tick, I wanted him to have a look at it.

Now, guys in the SEAL teams are not shy about a lot of things, but asking another SEAL in your platoon to check your asshole is a difficult thing to do, even if he is your platoon corpsman; it just invites too many damn jokes. The Doc took out his flashlight and after checking out my butt area, he said, "Looks like the head of a snake is trying to come out of your ass, Billy. That is the biggest damn hemorrhoid I have ever seen!"

I said, "A hemorrhoid? What the hell is that, and what can you do about it?" Our corpsman said that I needed a tube of "Preparation H," but he did not have one. So the Doc recommended that I go to the drugstore in the nearby town and buy one. If I did not, the problem would only get worse.

The next day, when it started to get dark, my teammate Paul and I patrolled out of our operational area, and we headed to the nearby town that was only about 4 miles away. This town had a population of about 200 people. There we all were, muddy, smelly, faces painted, and armed. We walked into the drug store and the old druggist behind the counter did not even look surprised. He just looked at us and said, "Can I help you boys?"

I said, "Ah, yes sir, I would like some Preparation H, sir."

He handed me the box of Preparation H and said, "Damn things sure do hurt, don't they, son?"

"Yes sir, they do," I replied.

I stuck my hand in my pocket to pull out some cash but the druggist said, "Son, it's on the house. If you had to walk in here from wherever it is that you came from, you are in more need of that ointment than I am of your cash." I thanked him for his kindness, and we left the store. Paul and I patrolled to a secure area, where I could use my newly purchased ass ointment.

As I was squeezing the ointment up my butt, I kept thinking, I hope to God no one puts a spotlight on us. What a picture this would make, one guy with a gun on the lookout, and another with his pants down shoving a tube of Preparation H up his ass.

Chapter 29

PURPLE HEAD

When you are an instructor in the SEAL teams, it allows you to be creative in your choices for target materials that you want other SEAL team platoons to attack or to blow up. In preparation for the next SEAL platoon training cycle, Chris and I were sent out to pick up some target material that was to be used at one of our training sites. We had a flatbed truck, and some tie-down chains, and cargo straps that we used to secure a huge diesel generator and four large transformers that we were going to use as a power sub station, which a SEAL platoon was going to use as a target to blow up.

We were heading through the Laguna Mountains in southern California with our heavy load secured in the back of our truck. Chris was driving, and I was half sleeping on the passenger side. Chris took a sharp turn, and we both heard a loud "crack" that came from behind us. Chris yelled out that we were going to roll over. I looked out my passenger window, and I saw the road pavement coming closer to my passenger window as our truck, with its heavy load, began to roll over.

What seemed to take forever actually happened in just a few seconds. My legs were sticking outside the shattered windshield when we were upside down, and Chris yelled out for me to pull my legs in. Just as I pulled my legs in the top of the cab crushed in on us completely. Had my legs remained outside they would have been cut off (thanks, Chris). I heard Chris scream out in pain as the steering wheel crushed down on his lap.

We continued to roll over until we came to a complete stop. We got out of our seatbelts, and we both kicked on the passenger-side door until it flung open. We crawled out of the cab of the truck and laid down on the side of the road, looking at our smashed truck and the diesel generator, including the four transformers that were lying all over the road. We both felt lucky to be alive as our truck had stopped rolling, in the upright position, just short of a cliff that dropped 400 feet to the canyon below.

As we were both checking ourselves, I found that I was bleeding from my head and from my right leg. Chris was lying on the side of the road complaining of severe pain to his groin area where the steering wheel had crushed down on him. I undid his pants and I saw that his penis was a deep red color, and that it was swelling up. It was at that moment that a state trooper rolled up on our accident. He asked if I was okay, and I said, "Yes, but I think that my teammate here is in bad shape."

The state trooper walked over to Chris. Chris was still moaning in severe pain. The trooper said that he needed to pull down Chris's pants to inspect the area of pain that Chris was complaining about. When the state trooper pulled down Chris's pants, it revealed Chris's wounded penis. Upon seeing Chris's wounded penis, the state trooper gasped, "Oh my God!" I looked over at Chris's penis and saw that it was still swelling up. The head of his penis was as big as a major league baseball, and it was starting to turn a deep purple color.

The state trooper called for an ambulance, and when it arrived, we were both transported to the local hospital. As the doctor was stitching up the gashes in my head and my leg, I looked over at Chris in the emergency room next to me, and I could see Chris's exposed penis. It was now looking like the top of a baseball bat that was going to explode any second.

A female doctor who specializes in male genitals (figure the odds) came into the emergency room. When she started to handle Chris's penis, Chris said, "Doc, I don't care about the color, I just want you to keep it this size, okay?"

She looked at Chris, and in a flat sarcastic voice she said, "I guess not having a normal penis like the rest of the male population, you must look at this as God's gift to you. However, I am not God, and I do not perform miracles. So, when I am done with you, you will have the same small penis you always had."

Chris and I both laughed out loud. It was good to be seen by someone with our sense of humor. However, Chris's laughter soon turned into a moan of anguish when she took out a scalpel and said that she was going to remove a large portion of his penis. Chris began to plead with her...

Again, it was her wonderful warped sense of humor, lucky for Chris.

Chapter 30

A FRIENDLY HOTEL IN ITALY

When it came to deploying for a SEAL mission, Walter and I were always volunteering. So when we heard about an operation in Italy that needed field radio communicators, we both jumped at the chance to go there. Having been accepted, we were both sent on the deployment to Italy for the purpose of establishing a clandestine radio communication relay site for a larger operation that was going to involve several SEAL platoons. Both of us had a background in clandestine communications, and we selected a mountain site that had some old ruins on top of it. This mountain location would afford us a good tactical position to set up our communications equipment, and the ruins would conceal our equipment and radio antennas from view by ground or air units. At the base of this mountain was a small town named San Felice. The town was small, and it had only one hotel. Nevertheless, the hotel was near our communications operating area, so we both thought it would be a great place to stay, as opposed to driving 23 miles to a different hotel that was located in another town.

When my partner and I went to the hotel to ask for a room, we were greeted by some strange stares. I asked if there was a problem, and the owner of the small hotel said that he did not rent rooms to gay men. This should have been my first clue as to what kind of a place this was where we were trying to get a room, but we were both tired and suffering from jet lag, and a hotel room with a bed for each of us was our top priority. After reassuring the owner that we were indeed straight, we told him that we needed two rooms for three weeks.

Oddly enough, this statement really caused a lot of confusion; it seems that they only rented rooms by the half hour or full hour, and because of this, the owner was not sure how to charge us. I looked at my teammate and said, "Who the hell rents a room by the hour?"

My teammate just shrugged his shoulders and said, "I guess they do."

I said, "Well, there are 24 hours in a day, how much could it be?" I told the owner that when we were in Rome, we paid 150 U.S. dollars per night, which included breakfast. He said that he would charge us the same rate, and he would have breakfast brought to us each morning. The rooms were very basic as hotel rooms go. There was a bed and a bathroom, no other furniture, and no TV or mini bar. However, there was entertainment in the form of moans, groans, screams, and beds banging against the walls all through the night.

As sleep was out of the question, my teammate Walter and I walked down to the nearby bar to consume a few liquid sleeping pills. It was at this bar and after a few drinks with the locals that we found out about the type of hotel that we were staying at: It was a bordello.

The locals all thought that it was amusing that we would try to sleep at a hotel filled with whores and people having one-night stands. After the first week, we both started to look like zombies, so we asked the local bartender if it was possible to rent a room from someone in town. He said that he would ask around for us, and let us know.

The next day, after working all day in the rain at the communications site, Walter and I went to the local bar. The bartender said that he had great news for us. It seems that a local farmer was willing to let us sleep in his barn, free of charge, if we did not mind doing a little work for him. Later that same night we both met the local farmer. He was a pleasant elderly gentleman, and he said that he would be happy to have us stay in his barn, and in return all we needed to do was to keep it clean for him. He also wanted us to do a little minor work for him like chopping for fires and feeding his horses.

Now, maybe shoveling crap sounds like a bad deal to some of you people reading this book, but let me tell you that our lack of sleep in that whorehouse made the barn sound like a penthouse suite! We took the farmer's generous offer. We were dry, it was warm, free, peaceful, and the air (when the horses did not flatulate) was fresh, and for breakfast, the farmer gave us great-tasting strong coffee with a huge chunk of bread, and a brick of cheese.

Now that barn was a great bed and breakfast hotel!

Chapter 31

SWIMMING IN CIRCLES UNDERWATER AND AT NIGHT

Night training dives in the SEAL teams can be a rather boring event. You slide into the cold water from a boat several miles offshore, take a bearing with your compass to your intended target, and submerge. You swim with your dive buddy to your intended target on a designated compass bearing with your rebreathing rigs, attach your explosives to various key points on the vessel, and after you have attacked your target, you take a reverse bearing and swim back out to sea, where hopefully you will get picked up. As always, it is dark, wet, and cold.

Occasionally (if you are not the guy concentrating on the compass and depth gauge), you might get to see something that created a huge phosphorescent glow go right past you, and you think to yourself, "That was big; hope it doesn't come back. However, if it does, I will grab my swim buddy and put him between me and whatever that big glowing thing is!" Hey, when danger comes to you at night and underwater, it sucks to be the compass diver.

Anyway, while on one of these many boring training diving missions (as I have said before, boredom is the mother of all inventions and practical jokes), I got the idea to mess around with my dive buddy. I brought along a powerful magnet and a bunch of extra lead dive weights. When we launched from the boat, my dive buddy (Doug) took a compass bearing to our target, and we submerged for the long underwater swim to our designated target.

After about 30 minutes into our dive, I carefully took out one of my 4-pound lead weights and placed it gently on his back. As we were wearing wetsuits, he did not feel the added weight. I heard him add air from his pure oxygen bottle to adjust for the increased weight on his body. I took out another 4-pound lead weight and carefully placed it on his back; again I heard him adjust for the added weight by adding more air into his rebreathing bags so that he could maintain the proper diving depth.

When my diving buddy had adjusted himself to the added weight, I quickly took both weights off his back. When I did this, he started to shoot towards the surface because of all the extra air that he put in his breathing bags to compensate for the extra weight, which was now gone. I pulled on our buddy line (this was about a 4 or 5 foot line that is attached between two divers) to keep him from breaking the surface of the water, which would have given away our position. I squeezed his arm once to ask if he was okay, and he squeezed my arm back to say yes. It was funny because Doug prided himself on being so professional on night compass swims.

After another 30 minutes had passed, I felt that it was now time for my powerful magnet. I took out my magnet, and I slowly moved it next to the compass. As the compass needle turned towards the force of the magnet, so did we underwater. I knew that we were going to be swimming way off course, but what the hell — this was fun. We swam for about an hour, and then we surfaced for a quick peek, only to find that we were nowhere near our target, and as a matter of fact, we were swimming out to sea!

The safety boat from which we had started our mission came over to us and asked if we were all right. I removed my regulator from my mouth and said, "Hell no, this guy is swimming in circles!"

Doug replied, "I don't know what the hell is wrong, this never happens to me. Maybe this compass is messed up." The guys in the safety boat checked the compass and of course, it was fine.

I looked at Doug and said, "You are like a new guy underwater! You had a hard time maintaining your depth, I had to pull you down to keep you from breaking the surface of the water, and look, we are not even anywhere near our target. Next time I will do the driving, because you suck!"

Doug was clearly upset with himself as we failed to hit our target. After the training mission, we all went to the bar that same night just to have a few brews before going home. As I was sitting there with Doug, he was feeling really bad. So I told Doug what I had done to him. Doug looked at me and said, "You are an asshole!"

Yup, that's me, Doug.

Chapter 32

YOU'RE ON THE NEWS

When you serve in the SEAL teams as a SEAL, you always want to stay away from the NEWS people as much as possible. The reason is that the NEWS people, for the most part, have their own self-serving agenda, and they could really care less about the real truth of what matters in their stories, or the events that "they" are reporting about, because it is their network ratings that rule, and not the real truth. After all, there is nothing like the sight of blood, guts, and gore to get the attention of the viewing audiences. The truth about what happened doesn't really matter; what matters is that everyone tunes in to their network to see all that carnage, and anyone that was a part of or responsible for it.

When I was deployed overseas as an advisor/trainer, I was returning from one of our many all-day training evaluations at the rifle range with a group of commandos. I was stunned as I watched this female reporter and her cameraman running up to confront me. I guess she thought that she had the scoop of the year, when she looked at me and said into her microphone, "Here we have it, positive proof that U.S. troops are engaged in combat operations in this country! What do you have to say about it, soldier?"

First off, I was thinking, I am not a soldier, and I was also thinking that I would like to take that microphone and shove it up her arrogant ass. I looked at her, and in a calm voice I said, "If you would please shut off the camera, and the tape recorder, I would like to make a statement first, and then I would be glad to give you an interview with me." She looked at the cameraman and told him to shut it off. I asked that he place the video camera on the hood of their vehicle with her recorder and microphone.

Once they both had done what I had asked, I turned to my men and said, "Arrest them, and put them in the holding area for prisoners of war." My men did what I asked, and they escorted this NEWS team away. The NEWS people were screaming and yelling obscenities at me as they were pushed into the back of the troop truck, and were transported to the enemy prisoner holding area.

I knew that these NEWS people were not authorized to be in our training area, because I had not received any contact from our military group commander about NEWS personnel visiting my location. So I picked up their video camera, and I took out the videotape and ripped the tape to pieces. I took out my 9mm pistol and shot a hole through the lens of the video camera; I then shot several more holes in the body of the camera itself. I picked up the reporter's audio recorder and tore out all the audiotape, and I smashed her tape recorder to pieces (it felt so good).

I was so pissed off at these NEWS people and their preconceived opinions, and their willingness to distort the truth in order to discredit U.S. military personnel without first obtaining any facts. I thought about just leaving them in the prisoner holding area for a few weeks without notifying anyone in my chain of command about them.

As I was in a generous mood (and they were Americans — although, in my opinion, of the lowest form), I called the U.S. embassy military group commander to report that I had two NEWS personnel in custody, and that I was holding them in our prisoner holding area. I also wanted to find out who these people were, and if they were given any special permission to be in my operational training area without first notifying me.

I was informed by my contact within the U.S. embassy that they did not have any permission or clearance papers to be in my operational area, and that a helicopter was going to be sent down to pick them up. I was further informed that once they were back at the U.S. embassy, they were going to be processed out of the country for violations of their agreement with the U.S. embassy.

I asked my contact if he could please delay the helicopter until nightfall, as I had them both inside an enemy prisoner holding area, and it would be a shame to release them so quickly. It was agreed that the helicopter would arrive just before nightfall.

I went to the enemy prisoner holding area where the reporter and cameraman were. I informed them that their video and audio equipment was being examined by the host country, and that they were both in violation of the armed force's agreement act with the host nation (whatever that was, but to me, it sounded good).

They both started yelling at me about the freedom of the press. I looked at them both and said, "This is not America, and your freedoms do not apply here. For your information, you are both going to be brought before a military tribunal and put on trial for propaganda crimes against this government. The supreme military commander of this base is preparing confession statements for the both of you to sign. Should either of you choose not to sign these papers, the commander advised me that the both of you will be taken by helicopter to a remote area where you will both be shot for sympathizing with the enemy, which in this country, just like in America, is treason."

The reporter said that I was full of shit, and that I was the one who was going to be in a lot of trouble for imprisoning them. I left them and went to see the base commander. When I arrived at the base commander's office, I told him what I had said to both of his unauthorized guests, and what I had planned for them about the helicopter. We both had a good laugh about it, and the commander could not resist going over to the enemy prisoner holding area to see them.

When the commander arrived at their cells, he started yelling and cussing at the both of them, and accusing them both of being enemy sympathizers, and that they had both committed high treason against his government and the people of his country. The commander told them that they were going to be flown to a remote area by helicopter where his execution squad would be waiting for them, and that after they were executed their bodies were to be left there to rot as a warning to all other enemy sympathizers. The base commander cursed at both of them again, and told his guards if they tried to escape, shoot them!

You should have seen their faces as the reality of the situation began to sink in. They had a complete change of attitude. They were now pleading with me to help them and to call the U.S. embassy to let the embassy know where they were. I said, "You belong to the commander of this base now, and not the U.S. embassy. You have no clearance papers to be here, you have been convicted of high treason against this government, and there is nothing that I can do for either of you." When I turned to leave them both, they were in tears, begging me, as a fellow American, to please help them.

After about three hours, I got a radio call informing me that the helicopter for the journalists was inbound; I went back to the enemy prisoner holding area with four armed guards. I opened up their cells and told them that I would escort them to the helicopter pad and take any last statements that they might want to give to their families.

They climbed into the back of the covered truck with the four armed guards and when we got to the helicopter pad, they climbed out of the truck, and stood there with their faces full of fear. I asked if they had any last words before they were to get onto the helicopter, and flown to their execution point. They were both crying and pleading with me to please save them. The guards motioned for them to get moving towards the helicopter. The reporter and the cameraman were both begging me to please help them, and that they would do anything for me if I would just help them (what a difference it makes, I thought, when THEY are the ones who need the help of the U.S. military). I said, "I have done everything that I can for the both of you. Now get on that damn helicopter, and try to die with some dignity."

The guards escorted them to the military helicopter, and as the helicopter crew was strapping them in with their safety harnesses, they saw that the helicopter crew were members of the U.S. military. They both looked at me and started yelling. I could not hear what they were saying because of the loud sounds that were coming from the helicopter's engines.

I did, however, completely understand both of their middle fingers that they were waving at me. I thought, Ahhh, it is so nice to be appreciated, and good riddance to a couple of complete losers!

Chapter 33

THE HARDER IT IS, THE MORE PAINFUL IT GETS

Sometimes, when a SEAL member is wounded, depending on the location of his wound and how he got it, it can be a lot of fun for the rest of his SEAL teammates. As it would happen, during a combat patrol mission in a faraway contested area of the world, Bob had to stop and answer one of nature's calls. It was while Bob was taking a crap that an enemy solider shot Bob in the ass. You have to admit that this particular enemy solider has the same warped sense of humor that almost all SEALs have.

After the firefight was over, and all of the SEALs had been extracted by boat, Bob was treated for his gunshot wound by the platoon corpsman. When Bob arrived at the field medical hospital, he was to learn the true extent of his injuries. The bullet had entered his right butt cheek, striking his pelvis bone, and continued on its path, exiting out through the side of his penis.

In order to save his penis, the doctors decided to send Bob back to the United States where a specialist would be able to treat the severity of this kind of wound. Before Bob arrived at the hospital in the States, the rumor was that an enemy sniper had shot off his penis. When Bob had finally arrived stateside, a friend informed him that his girlfriend had left him for another guy because he no longer had a penis. (Heck, it might not have been big, but I am sure it made Bob happy.)

After the surgery on Bob's penis was declared a success by the doctors, those of us that were in the States went to the hospital to see him. Bob told us that the doctors had to stitch up the entire length of his penis with 132 stitches. Of course, we all asked to see it, but it was all wrapped up with bandages that Bob did not want to remove just for us. We were all laughing and having a great time making comments about Bob's penis until the nurse came in and told us that Bob had to rest, and we would all have to leave.

The next day a few of us went back to the hospital to visit Bob. Bob asked the nurse how long he would have to wait before having sex. The nurse said that it would be several more weeks, because if his penis were to get hard, it would tear the stitches and possibly reopen his wound.

After hearing what the nurse said, we told Bob that we had some other places that we had to go to, and that we would see him again much later.

When we got down to the first floor, we all started laughing about an idea that we had: We would all go to downtown San Diego and pick up a prostitute for Bob (oh yeah). When we arrived at our destination, we picked up a prostitute, and we asked her if she was willing to indulge us in a practical joke. She said yes, and it would cost us 100 dollars for one hour. We asked her if she had a nurse's uniform, and she said, "Of course." So, we took her to her apartment where she changed into the nurse's outfit, and we all went over the plan as to what we wanted her to do.

When we got back to the hospital, we escorted our nurse up to Bob's room, and we told her that we would wait just outside his door while she went into Bob's room to do her "performance." Surprisingly, we did not have to wait long before we heard the loud screams of pain coming from inside Bob's room. Hearing Bob screaming, we all went inside and there was our nurse totally naked, and sensually playing with her body right next to Bob. Bob's penis was erect and oozing blood from his stitches, and of course, he was in a lot of pain from all the stitches tearing at the skin of his penis, as the harder it got, the more painful it got.

Bob's screams, however, did not go unnoticed by the real nurses who were working on the hospital floor. When the real nurses came running into Bob's room to see why he was screaming, they were astonished to find a totally naked woman next to Bob's bed, and not so astonished at seeing all of us standing there laughing.

The real nurses were extremely pissed off at us, and they started yelling at our "nurse" to put her clothes back on, and for all of us to get the hell out of Bob's room before they called the Shore Patrol (military police).

We told Bob that we would see him tomorrow, and that we were glad to see that his pecker was still in good working order. Bob did not respond to us as he had more pressing matters, lying there on his back moaning in pain, while the real nurses tended to his wounded, bleeding penis.

Chapter 34

OLD SEAL TEAM GUYS VS YOUNG SEAL TEAM GUYS

In the SEAL teams, the old SEALs always love how the young SEALs strut their stuff without any thought as to where the older SEALs might have been or what they might have done. Take a squad of seven men, two old SEAL team guys with five young SEAL pups/new guys, and sooner or later the young SEAL pups will try to flex their muscles around the old guys to impress them.

Out in the desert, our squad was formed to evaluate how long it would take a seven-man SEAL squad to patrol to a target, which in this case was a surface-to-air missile launching site, conduct a reconnaissance of the target, and then blow it up. After this, we would all patrol out to our designated pickup point. We were given five days to complete the mission. The one stipulation to this mission was that we were to start the mission with all of our water canteens empty. Any water that we needed, we were to "find" along the way if we wanted anything to drink.

We were to commence our mission after we all drank as much water as possible, and our urine was clear of any color. To start our mission, we were inserted thirty miles away from our target area, with food, our combat equipment, radios, and no water. At 5:00 p.m., we were dropped off at our insertion point, and we patrolled fast for about two hours before we took a short break.

It was during this break that the young SEAL pups let their alligator mouths overload their tadpole asses by saying to Bucky and me, "Do you think you two old guys will be able to keep up with us?"

"Yeah, we don't see any walkers out here that you two old guys can use."

"Hey, if you two old guys get tired, we can carry you the rest of the way."

Bucky and I looked at each other and nodded. We looked at the young SEAL pups and said, "Wait here, we are going to scout around for any signs of water." When Bucky and I got far enough away, we sat down and discussed a plan to put these young SEAL pups in their place. It was a simple plan, really: We were going to patrol non-stop to our target in one night. We both knew that we would also be hurting, but in the end, it was going to be worth it.

We arrived back at the location where we had left the young SEAL pups and said, "We didn't find any signs of water, so let's go." We were all patrolling at a fast pace, and we were not (according to our plan) going to take any breaks to look for water, eat food, or rest. It was not long before we heard one of the young SEAL pups say, "Are we going to stop and search for water?"

"No, keep moving," Bucky replied.

A short time passed, and yet again, another young pup said, "Can we stop for a short break?"

"No, we are going to keep moving," I said.

We were covering a lot of ground and if this had been a real mission, we would not be this careless, but as we were not in a foreign country and there were no real "bad guys," we stuck to our plan to punish these young smart asses. A couple of hours had passed, and one of the young pups said, "I need a break, can we stop?"

Bucky circled up our squad and said, "If you guys don't shut up and quit your damn crying, you can patrol back to the camp and quit. We are going to reach our target by morning, and we are not going to stop for anything or anyone." Bucky looked at me and said out loud, "I don't know what the f--k is coming out of BUD/S these days, but it isn't SEALs!"

We reached our target area just before dawn. We found an area that provided us all with cover and concealment, and I told the young SEAL pups to get some rest at this concealed area (lay up point), while Bucky and I went out and scouted around the area for any signs of water or the bad guys.

When Bucky and I were out of sight of the young SEAL pups, we found another spot that offered some concealment from any would-be bad guys. We took off our boots and aired out our feet, moaning and groaning from the pain we were in. We both rested there for a couple of hours and then we patrolled out to find some water. As luck would have it, we found a small crevasse that had a little water in it. It also had a live rattlesnake, and a dead and rotting jackrabbit covered with maggots.

Bucky killed the rattlesnake, and we decided to bring the jackrabbit as food for the young SEAL pups, so we scooped it out of the crevasse and put it inside one of our plastic bags. Bucky started to laugh as he cut off the head and tail of the rattlesnake and skinned it. Looking at me, Bucky smiled and said, "We're not done with those poor bastards yet." I watched as Bucky replaced the jackrabbit's intestines with the skinned rattlesnake. Bucky looked at me and said, "You and I are going to eat the snake, and nothing else." It was going to get hot out in the desert sun, and the smell from this rotting jackrabbit was going to be a bit overpowering for those young studs.

When we patrolled back to where we had left the young SEAL pups, all but one of them was asleep. Bucky threw the jackrabbit in the center where they all were and said, "This is everyone's lunch." We also told them that we had found some water, and that we would patrol back to it with everyone's canteens after we ate the jackrabbit. The young SEAL pups looked at the jackrabbit inside the plastic bag, and when one of them opened it, he gagged, saying that it was rotten and covered with maggots.

Bucky put on his disgusted face and said, "Is there no end to the whining of you new guys? Billy and I will eat the intestines from this jackrabbit, and the rest of the jackrabbit, you spoiled little new guys can have!"

One of the new guys said, "If you eat the intestines from that rotting rabbit, then we will eat the rest of that rabbit!"

"OK, you're on!" said Bucky.

Buck ripped out the intestines (rattlesnake meat) from the rabbit and said, "I will cook it up right now, and Billy and I will eat it." When Bucky was finished cooking the intestines/snake meat, the young SEAL pups stared at us in disbelief as we both ate all of it. When we finished our meal, Bucky said, "Give us your canteens, we are going to go fill them up, and while we are gone, you guys eat that rabbit!" We left them to their lunch and headed out to the spot where we found the water.

When we got back with everyone's water, we saw that they had burned the rabbit to a crisp before they ate it (hey, at least they ate some of it). Bucky looked at all of them and said, "One day, we 'old guys' won't be around to care for you young SEAL pups. So you might want to start thinking about listening to us, getting tough, or getting out!"

It was funny to see so many humble heads hanging low. If only they knew the truth! Well, now they do!

PHOTOS OF INTEREST

Taking a much-needed bath after a night in the field.

Bad guys are not around... Take 5.

I hate camels.

Western Pacific—love the jungle!

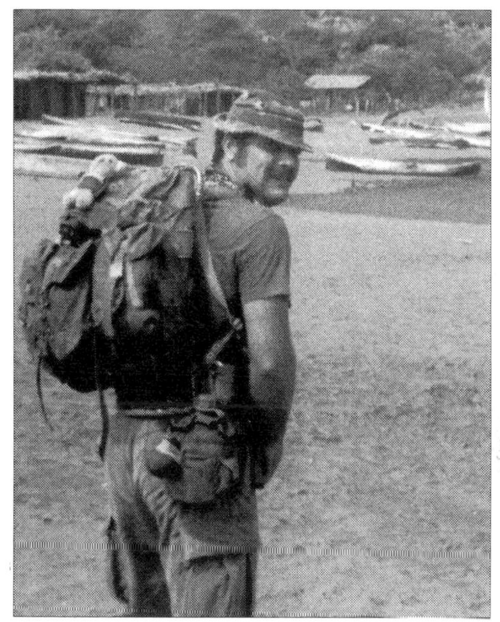

The teddy bear was for people in the platoon that complained a lot.

Gone... but never forgotten.

SEAL tridents covering the casket to honor our fallen SEAL brother.

CODE OF HONOR

Navy SEALs live by a code of honor, and it does not end when we leave the U.S. Navy SEAL Teams.

Never forget that you are a brother to ALL SEALs. Whatever you do solely, or together as a team, is not for any self-acknowledgment, or award.

All SEALs detest tyranny, and those who make their people suffer under absolute despotism. You were trained to help those who cannot help themselves, and to fight for those who cannot fight for themselves.

When you give your word, keep it. It is the essence of who you are. Tell the truth, even if it means that you will be prosecuted.

Never turn your back on an adversary; stand your ground.

In combat, kill the enemy as quickly as possible... Remember, like you, he has loved ones. He is someone's son, a father, a brother, an uncle, a cousin, or a friend... He is fighting hard for what he believes is right and just.... as are you.

Respect all those who show you respect.

You are honor bound to help ANYONE who is being oppressed at ANYTIME, by anyone. Never leave a brother SEAL behind.

Fight until you run out of bullets, take your enemy's weapon and use it against him, or fight with your knife... NEVER surrender.

Always stand by the will of the American People who have instilled their faith and trust in you to keep them free.

After any mission, never stand around waiting to be thanked for doing what is expected of you; make yourself ready for the next attack or mission.

The American Flag is our nation's banner, and it represents freedom, justice, and honor; never bring disgrace to it.

Your SEAL trident is your badge of honor; never bring disgrace to it or to any of those who have earned the right to wear it.

Never brag about what you have done on missions; it is/was a TEAM effort.

Fight hard, so that others will NOT have to return, and finish what you should have. NEVER lose faith in GOD.

Stay true to our Code of Honor...

A life spent fighting for others, who cannot fight for themselves, is a life worth living... and it is a noble life. Remember that only the weak of mind believe that what we do in battle, is who we are as men.

Remember, too, that in the fight against tyranny, every SEAL death has a worth, and every SEAL brother will surely know of it.

IN RETROSPECT

I know lots of SEALs that, when asked, would tell you that they have had a full life (and they are in their thirties and forties!). They did their jobs because they love their country, their families, and their teammates. They did not join the SEAL teams to earn medals; most of the SEAL team guys who I know rarely wore them, let alone talked about them. They are men of honor with a deep sense of loyalty and duty.

After all is said and done, most SEALs have seen, felt, and done things that few people on this planet will ever dream of. I believe that SEALs live more in one lifetime than most people would if they were given two lives to live. That old saying that "most people pass through life, but few people truly live life" applies to the men of the U.S. Navy SEAL teams.

As most SEALs burn the candle of life at both ends, perhaps this, too, explains why a good number of SEALs die in their late sixties. They are like shining stars in the night, burning ever so brightly, and then they are gone.

For some of you, you may think that being a U.S. Navy SEAL is cool, and you may want to seek that profession. If you do, you will not find it an easy life or path to follow. Knowing the serious nature of a SEAL's job, and all the realities that come with it, I can tell you that being a U.S. Navy SEAL is far from being "cool." It has always been easier to destroy than it is to create. Your life, and the lives of your brother SEALs, will be in jeopardy almost on a daily basis. You should aspire to be the best at whatever your chosen field/career is, but more importantly, you should aspire to be a noble person with honor.

It may be true what Thetis said to her son: "If you marry and live an ordinary life, you will be remembered by your sons and daughters, and their sons and daughters. However, in time, you will be forgotten. Such is the fate of all ordinary men."

However, and thankfully, there are thousands of "ordinary" men and women out there, and they are the unsung heroes who on a daily basis help people, save lives, care for a special child when others would not, fight the fight for others when they cannot, and keep their word when they give it, even if it means their demise.

To those heroes… I will always lift my glass in respect.

CLOSING REMARKS

Now that you have read the many stories within this book (and God knows how many there are left untold), I hope that you have gained some small measure of appreciation, and gained some insight as to why SEALs pull pranks, tell funny stories about those who have been injured or killed, and why SEALs, in general, look to find humor in tragedy. I have no deep philosophical explanation for what it means to be a Navy SEAL. However, after reading all of these stories, one can assume that it is a life filled with sacrifice, honor, and brotherhood.

For most of us who are/were Navy SEALs, it means serving with honor and with the greatest guys on earth.

There may be a variety of reasons as to why SEALs find humor in tragedy. However, the majority of the reasons might just be that for those of us who have served or are still serving in the SEAL teams, death has become all too familiar. We do not hate or fear death, because we all know that one day death will come for us and take us home to see all our brothers that have gone before us.

Those of us who have served or are serving in the SEAL teams keep our brothers alive within others and within ourselves through the stories that we all share about each other. I (like other SEALs) do not want our brothers to feel sorrow for us, should we be personally wounded, killed, or die of natural causes. We just want to be remembered for what we did together, and the fun times that we all shared as brothers in the SEAL teams.

As members of any U.S. Navy SEAL team, we all know that it is an honor, and a privilege, to serve our country. We also know that fighting for freedom leaves a taste in the mouth that the protected will never appreciate.

There are a few who will ridicule us for our service to our country. Those who ridicule our chosen career will never know how much was sacrificed, or all the footprints that we left behind on countless accomplished missions all over the world on their behalf so that all of us may keep our right to freedom of speech and to live free from being oppressed.

ACKNOWLEDGEMENTS

To all the Frogmen and SEALs that have gone to the other side ahead of us, let us never forget them, and let us honor them by telling their funny stories as often as we can, and to all who will listen.

To all those whom I have come to know and call my brothers or friends (very few that you are), to those of you who have dedicated your time and efforts to encourage me to write this book.

To those of you who assisted me in the structuring of this book, and kept me focused on what it was that I was trying to achieve with my writing, I thank you for your blunt honesty.

I give a very special thank you to:

- Ellen Reid, President
  Ellen Reid's Book Shepherding
  (www.indiebookexpert.com)

- Pamela Cangioli
- The SEAL Foundation
  nswfoundation.org
- The Navy SEAL Museum
  navysealmuseum.com
- The Navy SEAL Fund
  http://www.navysealsfund.org
- The UDT SEAL Association
  udt-seal-association.org
- The SEAL Legacy Foundation
  https://www.seallegacy.org
- America's Mighty Warriors
  http://americasmightywarriors.org/_a/

To all of you who have assisted me when I was unable to help myself, you have earned my undying admiration and respect.

And to all of you who have read or purchased this book, I thank you. If this book made you smile, and realize that SEALs love to enjoy life, then I have achieved my purpose in writing this book.

www.billyallmonauthor.com

Made in the USA
San Bernardino, CA
20 February 2016